Art and Political Thought in
Bole Butake

Art and Political Thought in Bole Butake

Emmanuel N. Ngwang and
Kenneth Usongo

LEXINGTON BOOKS
Lanham • Boulder • New York • London

Published by Lexington Books
An imprint of The Rowman & Littlefield Publishing Group, Inc.
4501 Forbes Boulevard, Suite 200, Lanham, Maryland 20706
www.rowman.com

Unit A, Whitacre Mews, 26-34 Stannary Street, London SE11 4AB

We are grateful to Professor Bole Butake and the original publisher for not only granting
us an interview, but also for consenting to it to be published and authorizing us to quote
extensively from his plays.

British Library Cataloguing in Publication Information Available

Library of Congress Cataloging-in-Publication Data

Names: Ngwang, Emmanuel N., author. | Usongo, Kenneth, author.
Title: Art and political thought in Bole Butake / Emmanuel N. Ngwang and Kenneth Usongo.
Description: Lanham : Lexington Books, 2016. | Includes bibliographical references and index.
Identifiers: LCCN 2016030390 (print) | LCCN 2016032214 (ebook) | ISBN 9781498538107 (cloth :
    alk. paper) | ISBN 9781498538114 (Electronic)
Subjects: LCSH: Butake, Bole--Criticism and interpretation. | Cameroonian drama--History and criti-
    cism.
Classification: LCC PR9372.9.B87 Z77 2016 (print) | LCC PR9372.9.B87 (ebook) | DDC 822--dc23
    LC record available at https://lccn.loc.gov/2016030390

∞™ The paper used in this publication meets the minimum requirements of American
National Standard for Information Sciences Permanence of Paper for Printed Library
Materials, ANSI/NISO Z39.48-1992.

Printed in the United States of America

Contents

Acknowledgments

We are grateful to Professor Bole Butake for not only granting us an interview, but also for consenting to it to be published and authorizing us to quote extensively from his plays. Thank you to Editions CLE, Butake's publisher, for permission to quote excerpts of his writings.

We were privileged to work with an excellent editorial staff at Lexington Books. Kate Tafelski and Carissa Marcelle were timely in responding to our inquiries and exemplary in facilitating the publication of this book. Finally, we commend our spouses, Susana and Mira, for believing in this book project.

ONE

Contextualizing Butake

Introduction

Even though the birth of Anglophone Cameroon literature is often traced to Sankie Maimo's publication of *I am Vindicated* (1959), this assessment is limited to written literature and does not take into consideration various indigenous literatures that existed in oral form long before Maimo's book. These oral expressions were in the forms of folktales, myths, legends, dirges, riddles, epics, and chants. Anglophone Cameroon literature has grown out of particular historical, political and social circumstances. Although early Anglophone Cameroon literature (1950s and 1960s) seems to have been more preoccupied with showcasing the cultural values of English-speaking Cameroonians, contemporary Anglophone Cameroon literature has rarely overlooked foregrounding the downtrodden state of Anglophones in Cameroon against the majority Francophones. Pioneer Anglophone writers such as Sankie Maimo, Mbella Sonne Dipoko, and Kenjo Jumbam, for example, appear to have premised their art essentially on cultural identity as well as exploring the relationship between the European colonizer and the African colonized.

However, politically committed literature became preeminent when writers like Bate Besong and Victor Epie Ngome, in a revolutionary tone, started dramatizing the political, economic, and social mistreatment of English-speaking Cameroonians by their French-speaking counterparts. This creative trajectory appears foundational in Anglophone Cameroon literature in that artists like Bole Butake, John Nkemngong Nkengasong, Mbuh Mbuh, and John Ngong Kum have been unwavering in denouncing, in their art, the barefaced political, economic, and social deprivations experienced by Anglophones in Cameroon. The emphasis in this burgeoning literature is mainly on the despicable effects of what some peo-

1

ple refer to as the Anglophone Problem, which means Anglophone Cameroonians are roundly discriminated against and condescended upon by Francophones, especially in matters of administration, economic development and culture.

The contention in *Art and Political Thought in Bole Butake* is that Butake's drama symbolically mirrors some of the abuses like corruption, misuse of power, marginalization, female (dis)empowerment prevalent in Cameroon, as well as envisages protest and courage as methods of redressing the status quo. By analyzing Butake's drama against the current sociopolitical realities of Cameroon, we intend to shed light on the complexities of his art and pinpoint correlations between it and his society. Cameroon is symbolic of several nations in Africa, in particular, and the world, in general, that nurture and sustain injustices. It is partly this unfortunate reality that ignited the creative stimulus in the famed Butake, whom we are proud and privileged to introduce to the reader.

Let us begin by familiarizing ourselves with Bole Butake as an academician as well as understanding, in detail, the historical context that informs his writing. The playwright Bole Butake was born in Nkor, North West Region of Cameroon, in 1947. Upon graduating from the local primary school, Butake attended Sacred Heart College, Mankon, and then CCAST Bambili. He later enrolled at the University of Yaoundé 1, Cameroon, where he obtained a Bachelor's degree. Thereafter, he earned a Master's degree in English from the University of Leeds, England, and a doctorate from the University of Yaoundé 1, where he lectured for many years, retiring as a professor of African literature in 2012. Butake combined teaching and scholarship, publishing many creative works and authoring scores of peer-reviewed essays both nationally and internationally.

However, Butake captured national and international attention and established his reputation as a dramatist in the publication and production of works like *Lake God, And Palm Wine Will Flow, The Survivors, Shoes and Four Men in Arms, Dance of the Vampires,* and *The Rape of Michelle*—mainly in terms of their political underpinnings. By opting for a study of his plays, we intend to place his imaginative universe within the sociopolitical matrix of Cameroon and demonstrate the topicality of the issue of governance in, for example, Cameroon or Africa that Butake consistently foregrounds in his creative works.

Although Butake often anchors his imagery in the Noni society (northwest region) of Cameroon, one can argue that he uses this artistic platform to make political commentary on Cameroon. Put differently, the Grassfields in his dramaturgy is a literary prism to gauge the sociopolitical situation of the country. It is important for the reader to note that Cameroon has had a protracted history of colonization. First colonized by Germany at the Berlin Conference of 1884–1885, the country was later subjected to French and British rule after the defeat of Germany in World

War I. While the French annexed the larger section east of the Mungo river, the British administered the smaller section west of the same river. These two territories are usually referred to respectively as La République du Cameroun or East Cameroon and West Cameroon or Southern Cameroons.

La République du Cameroun gained its independence from France in 1960. A year later, following a plebiscite in 1961, West Cameroon voted to achieve independence from Britain by unifying with East Cameroon to become the Federal Republic of Cameroon. This transition was the result of two flawed options presented to Southern Cameroonians by the United Nations, namely, achieving independence either by being absorbed by Nigeria or be fused with La République du Cameroun. The ideal option of sovereignty for Southern Cameroons was ignored partly because of Britain's unwillingness to support it primarily because of the fear that Southern Cameroons was believed to be economically weak and so might be a burden to Her Majesty's treasury. A treasury, we all remember, that flourished on the spoils of colonialism.

Immediately after unification, both territories (La République du Cameroun and Southern Cameroons) were run as federated states with separate political, educational, and judicial systems. However, in 1972, President Ahmadou Ahidjo orchestrated a change that coalesced the two states into a unitary system of governance and renamed the country as the United Republic of Cameroon. Ahidjo's successor, President Paul Biya, in 1984, with the stroke of the pen, renamed the country the Republic of Cameroon, reverting to the 1961 nomenclature that had been reserved to the French-speaking Cameroon. Interestingly, in terms of political governance, if Ahidjo gained notoriety for his ruthlessness reminiscent of Shakespeare's Macbeth, Biya is distinguished for his guile, the modern equivalence of Iago.

The merger of West Cameroon (Southern Cameroons) with East Cameroon has provoked much unrest among English-speaking Cameroonians. Granted that East Cameroon was generally governed through the French colonial policy of assimilation which prided itself in making French-speaking Cameroonians speak, dress, walk, and dance like the French, West Cameroon experienced a British colonial policy of indirect rule whereby Anglophones exercised some leverage of autonomy in matters of politics, education, culture and the judiciary.

Unfortunately, the establishment of a unitary system of governance in Cameroon was achieved at a high cost to the West Cameroonians, for the arrangement mainly integrated aspects of French colonial administration, reversing the equal status of both states to one of subservience where the West Cameroonians found themselves in a helpless situation of subjugation and servitude to the majority Francophones, a de facto form of internal colonization. As John Nkemngong Nkengasong pointedly observes, the "French colonial legacy overwhelmingly dominate[d] national life and therefore, consciously (or unconsciously) annihilates the socio-cultural, economic and political culture of Anglophones, acquired from their experience as members of a former British colony."[1] Anglophones generally see themselves as victims of internal colonialism given, for example, the predominance of French language over English in official business, the exclusive reserve of political offices like the president of the republic and several other key administrative appointments as the preserve of Francophones.

Anglophone Cameroonians have always been subjected to various forms of political and economic deprivations at the hands of their Francophone counterparts. For example, in 1992, a State of Emergency was imposed on the North West Region in Cameroon by President Paul Biya because of a contested presidential election, and this arbitrary declaration resulted in the deaths, torture, rape, and incarceration of so many innocent people. Furthermore, there have been systematic attempts by the Francophone-led government in Cameroon to cripple or abort economic ventures such as the Marketing Board, PowerCam, to name a few, in the North West and South West Regions of Cameroon. In this regard, the frustrations of Anglophone Cameroonians were succinctly stated in Dr. John Ngu Foncha's resignation letter to Paul Biya, chairman of the CPDM (Cameroon People's Democratic Movement). It should be recalled that Foncha was the architect of the unification of the two Cameroons. Among several grievances addressed in his letter dated June 9, 1990, Foncha laments that:

> All projects of the former West Cameroon I had either initiated or held very dear to my heart had to be taken over, mismanaged and ruined, e.g. Cameroon Bank, West Cameroon Marketing Board, WADA in Wum, West Cameroon Cooperative Movement. . . . All the roads in West Cameroon my government had either built, improved or maintained were allowed to deteriorate making Kumba-Mamfe, Mamfe-Bamenda, Bamenda-Wum-Nkambe, Bamenda-Mom inaccessible by road. Projects were shelved even after petrol produced enough money for building them and the Limbe sea port.

Furthermore, when the leaders of a political party defied a heavy government crackdown and launched the opposition party the Social Democratic Front (SDF) in Bamenda on May 26, 1990, Cameroon Radio and Television (CRTV) inflamed an already politically charged situation by claiming that sympathizers of the party sang the Nigerian national anthem and even labeled the party's supporters "Biafrans." Biafra, it should be stated, is a reference to the southeastern part of Nigeria, which attempted to break away from the rest of the country by engaging in a civil war from 1967–1970.

The multiple injustices inflicted on Anglophone Cameroonians have led to the creation of pressure and activist groups such as the AAC (All

Anglophone Conference) and the SCNC (Southern Cameroons National Council). While the one held two meetings in Buea and Bamenda in 1993 and 1994 respectively to draw government's attention to the discriminations perpetuated against Anglophones, the other is engaged in a pacific struggle for the independence of Southern Cameroons from La République du Cameroun. Nowadays, many Anglophones believe that the transition from British colonial rule to a union with East Cameroon is tantamount to escaping from the paws of a leopard only to fall into the fangs of a lion.

As a nation, Cameroon is saddled with numerous political and social abuses. It is either the question of the incarceration of political activists, nepotism, or one of endemic corruption that has eroded the moral fabric of the country. It is against this backdrop of political and social injustices that Bole Butake's wrote his plays. It should be noted these plays are pure literature and come fully enriched with the values and characteristics of dramaturgy and dramatic literature. Hence, our approach to the plays is not necessarily political, but it cannot avoid the political because the plays are set within a geopolitical environment that provides each play the character types, themes, language and setting for the subject matter.

Much of the scholarship on Anglophone Cameroon literature has been general, analyzing the creative works of major writers without focusing on one main author to better showcase his or her literary aesthetics and motifs. This critical direction has been embraced by critics such as Emmanuel Fru Doh in *Anglophone-Cameroon Literature: An Introduction*, where he studies selected works of poetry, drama, and prose to indicate their preoccupation with the political marginalization of Anglophones. This same theme is taken up by Joyce B. Ashuntantang in *Landscaping Postcoloniality: The Dissemination of Cameroon Anglophone Literature* wherein she argues that Anglophone Cameroon literature deserves more critical attention because of its coming of age. Similarly, Shadrach Ambanasom's *Education of the Deprived: Anglophone Cameroon Literary Drama*, while emphasizing the neglect of this literature, also undertakes a perceptive analysis of major Anglophone Cameroon dramatists.

Art and Political Thought in Bole Butake seeks to center the literary argument on one main writer because this approach, unlike the above-cited studies that appear encyclopedic, would better accentuate the artistic merits of the writer. Our critical stance that entails a close reading of one main Anglophone Cameroon writer constitutes a major break from the critical tradition that has always yoked Anglophone Cameroon authors, with limited room for in-depth analysis. By shifting the thrust of literary argumentation from major authors to one author, we are moving the focus, in metaphorical terms, from the forest to the tree. Apart from a doctoral dissertation at the University of Witwatersrand (South Africa) by Naomi Epongse Nkealah entitled "Challenging Hierarchies in Anglophone Cameroon Literature: Women, Power and Visions of Change in

Bole Butake's Plays" (2011) that explores ways through which Butake empowers women and Oscar Labang's *Riot in the Mind: A Critical Study of John Nkemngong Nkengasong* (2008) that demonstrates Nkengasong's preoccupation with issues of corruption and power abuse in Cameroon, this study is the third published critical work entirely centered on a notable Anglophone Cameroon dramatist.

This text *Art and Political Thought in Bole Butake* opens by situating Butake within a historical context that feeds his creative imagination. This is followed by an interview granted by Bole Butake in 2003. In this insightful conversation, he explains his focus on writing drama in terms of his intent to dialogue directly with his audience as well as his resolve to conscientize the marginalized Cameroonian masses mainly on some of the political and social deprivations to which they have been subjected. At the same time, Butake is worried about the greed and egocentricity of the ruling class in a society that has set up a coercive military and gendarmerie to intimidate people and minimize any opposition to the regime's quest to despoil the wealth of the nation. He comments, among other concerns, on the influence of writers such as Chinua Achebe, Wole Soyinka, Ngugi wa Thiong'o, and Athol Fugard on his creativity and bemoans the political bickering among Anglophone leaders and pressure groups in the jostle for influence and power. By so doing, Butake places himself on the same platform with literary giants and activists who have often used literature as a platform for revolt, a mirror of the society to reflect the ills of distorted dreams. And coming after independence, Butake becomes the postcolonial voice flagellating his society, bewailing the loss of the Edenic past and the introduction of political systems which are at variance with genuine democracy and have instead given rise to corruption and selfishness.

Chapter 3 of this book is centered essentially on politics in Butake's *And Palm Wine Will Flow, The Rape of Michelle,* and *Lake God.* These three plays depict a society under the siege of evils such as misuse of power, nepotism, tribalism, and corruption. These plays have their roots in actual sociopolitical events such as calls for a sovereign national conference and multi-party democracy that especially rocked Cameroon in the 1990s. It is argued that Butake's drama mainly constitutes a critique of the regime of President Paul Biya of Cameroon, which has become, in a Hamletian manner, a long index of unfulfilled or deferred promises on political and social changes. Throughout the plays, there is the impression of a battle between the oppressors, on the one hand, and the oppressed, on the other, and the playwright aligns with the latter.

As a sequel to the idea of the polarization of Cameroon, the chapter "Re-Configuring of Colonialism in Postcolonial Cameroon in Bole Butake's Plays" appraises the legacy of the colonial experience in Africa, in general, and Cameroon, in particular. Political leadership on the continent is shown as a vestige of colonial lingering of assimilation, with leaders who seem more preoccupied with serving the interest of Europe rather than Africa. Added to the issue of neocolonialism is the situation, as decried by Shey Ngong in Butake's *And Palm Wine Will Flow*, where meritocracy gives way to mediocrity and leaders lord over the ruled. Unfortunately, leaders also cultivate a cult of worship around themselves, arrogating such honorific titles as the Holy one and the lion of Ewawa. Their grip on power is facilitated by a subservient and ruthless military or police that distinguishes itself in brutality and corruption.

Chapter 5 undertakes a comparison of the colonial legacy and the culture of corruption in *Lake God* and *The Rape of Michelle*. Butake's plays depict leaders who do whatever is possible to maintain their grip on power; these leaders expend their energies devising and refining their newfound culture of corruption while ignoring the suffering of the marginalized masses. While in rural areas, Butake appeals for the overthrow of such dictators, in urban centers this message appears undercut by the powerful machinery of the politicians who connive with the judiciary to fend off any opposition to their rule. Corruption in Butake's plays is compared to the situation in Victor Musinga's *The Tragedy of Mr. No-Balance*. Although the protagonist in the latter play ends up being incarcerated, his bribery escapades, like those of Butake's characters, demonstrate how deeply rooted corruption is in Cameroon.

In chapter 6, "Female Empowerment and Political Change in *Lake God, The Survivors,* and *And Palm Wine Will Flow*," the contention is that the dramatist alters the traditional duty of the fight for political liberation which has often been the realm of the men to women. Women are depicted as leading the task for liberating the society from oppression and other forms of subjugation. As one examines Butake's plays, there is the suggestion that women, in his native Cameroon, enjoy extraordinary powers which have simply been submerged, if not totally stifled, by the male-oriented society, a society that has circumscribed women to seemingly subordinate roles like household keeping and procreation. His coded message is that faced with the political ineptitude which has often been manifested by men in positions of authority in Africa, women should be given a chance at governance.

Chapter 7 of the text entitled "Symbol and Meaning in *Lake God and Other Plays*" posits that Butake's drama constitutes an indictment of the social, political and economic injustices experienced by most underprivileged people at the hands of a strong minority. Using the explosion of Lake Nyos (Cameroon) in 1986, Butake constructs socially and politically charged plays that interrogate contemporary issues like leadership, human rights and citizenship, democracy, female empowerment, and good management of community property not only in Cameroon, but wherever there is injustice. He uses such crucial symbols as the *Fibuen, Kwifon,* cattle, *kibaranko,* vampire, and shoes in order to question some of the ills of his society. At the same time, Butake proposes ways such as protest or disobedience to end the exploitation and oppression of the masses by insensitive and avaricious elite.

The focus in chapter 8 is on elements of orality such as proverbs, honorific greetings, cults, rituals, and divinations to show how in the play *Lake God* Butake employs them not only as a display of the rhetoric of Noni people, but fundamentally to illuminate character, demonstrating the conflicting choices confronting his protagonists as well as alluding to the gray boundary between Christianity and traditional African religion. Butake's interpolation of elements of oral literature in his craft equally exemplifies the affinities between the oral and written literatures of Africa.

Chapter 9, "Character and the Supernatural in *Lake God*," approaching *Lake God* through a New Historicist framework, discusses Butake's main characters in this play—the Fon, Father Leo, Shey Bo-Nyo, and Angela—indicating that he foregrounds their character traits against the backdrop of traditional Noni religion, as well as Christianity. Thus, the bigotry and belligerence of both the Fon and Father Leo, for example, are projected through a supernatural frame.

Finally, the book explores, in chapter 10, the aesthetics of Butake's creativity within the context of governance in Africa. Butake's oeuvre continues to inspire so many people: from disenfranchised groups that see in his drama a path to reclaiming liberties and to critics who are challenged to hone their literary tools in the endeavor to situate his works within the dynamics of politics and culture in Africa. To this end, this study wraps up with a select annotated bibliography on Butake to indicate trends in his critical appraisal.

NOTE

1. John Nkemngong Nkengasong, "Interrogating the Union: Anglophone Cameroon Poetry in the Postcolonial Matrix." *Journal of Postcolonial Writing* 48.1 (2012), 52.

TWO

Interview with Professor Bole Butake, Dramatist and University Professor who Refused to Be "Lapiroed" [1]

E. N. Ngwang: What attracted you to drama/theatre rather than to short stories and novels or poetry?

Prof. Butake: My interest in creative writing actually began with the writing of poetry. I have a collection of some twenty-five and more poems which were composed up to about 1980. Many of them were actually published in *The Mould: A Magazine of Creative Writing*, which I and a group of undergraduate students at the University of Yaoundé published from 1976–1981 after which my poetry publication ceased. At the time that I was writing poetry, I also wrote some short stories such as "The Mad Man and the Healthy Dog," "Nkiendah's Red Eyes," "The Way of the City," "Betrothal without Libation," etc. Two of my short stories were published in *Calalloo* in the United States way back in the 1980s. I even wrote a novel, *The Luncheon*, which has never been published. So you see, I actually began by writing poetry, short stories, and a novel.

But I had to move away from poetry and prose because I needed to communicate, to dialogue with an audience. Poetry and the short story could not give me that opportunity because of very low readership. I needed a genre that would put me in direct contact with the audience and that is why I started writing plays. My first play, in fact, was a transformation of one of my short stories, *Betrothal without Libation*, which is still unpublished. In this regard, December 1984 is a very significant date and milestone for me because at that time I participated in an international workshop in Kumba (southwest Cameroon) on Theatre for Inte-

9

grated Rural Development. This workshop helped me to realize the communicative capabilities and great impact of theatre.

E. N. Ngwang: How many plays have you written so far? And what central themes or subjects have you grappled with in your plays?

Prof. Butake: So far I have seven published plays, the most recent one being *Zintgraff and the Battle of Mankon* (with Gilbert Doho, 2003*). Lake God and other Plays* (Editions CLE, 1999) which includes *The Survivors, And Palm wine Will Flow, Shoes and Four Men in Arms, Dance of the Vampires,* and *The Rape of Michelle.* My major concern was to conscientize the ordinary marginalized Cameroonian masses who are suffering the burdens of poverty and deprivation of their basic human rights by a ruthless, nonchalant and absolutely repressive regime that has surrendered itself to French neo-colonialism. But I think it is important to point out that I have done a good number of scenarios either on request or for specific purposes such as workshop situations.

Many of these scripts have been done either by myself or in collaboration with others, especially Gilbert Doho. Many have been filmed and screened on CRTV (Cameroon Radio and Television), especially for the program "Women and Development." Examples include *Grung Palaver, The Bride Price, Wanted: Another Son, The Business Woman, Horse Game, Survival Tactics, Hard Road to School, Death for All in the New Millenium, Chop a Chop, Nyang-HIV/AIDS,* and with Gilbert Doho, *L'éxciseuse de Pouss, Kam No Go, Alien in my Land, L'Instituteur d'Eyala, Mantrobo.* In the last seven or eight years, most of my theatre work has been oriented towards what I call A People's Theatre and People's Cinema, in which I use theatre for development methodology to conscientize people at grassroots with regard to their rights and responsibilities in the country, Cameroon.

E. N. Ngwang: What do you consider to be the greatest challenges and objectives the Cameroonian playwright (and by extension, the African playwright) faces and must overcome or accomplish respectively, as he or she goes about the business of writing or reaching his or her audience?

Prof. Butake: To my mind, the greatest challenge the Cameroonian playwright faces is to be able to prick the consciences of the governing bureaucratic élites who see themselves as overlords rather than as servants of the Cameroonian people. This is a very crucial point. The ruling class in Cameroon is made up of a band of absolutely greedy and self-centered vultures who neither believe in the nation called Cameroon nor in the various ethnicities who constitute the population of that country. So they have invented all types of diabolic strategies to keep Cameroonians at loggerheads with each other while they continue to despoil the wealth of the nation. They have set up the armed forces (the military, gendarmerie, police) against the very populations that their duty commands them to protect. The judiciary has allowed itself to be pocketed by the executive. The legislature is controlled and dominated by the RDPC[2] (ruling party), which does not have the guts to hold any dialogue with its president who also doubles as the chairman of the party and president of the Republic. The administration is unproductive, thoroughly corrupt, and over-centralized. The educational system, the key and nucleus of any potential for progress and development, is moribund, outmoded, neglected in terms of infrastructure and personnel, with curricula that are as goalless as the certificates are worthlessly ill-adapted to the developmental needs of the citizens.

However, since the lords are unredeemable, the only other option is to focus on raising the awareness of the marginalized, subjugated, and impoverished masses to enable them to take their destinies into their own hands by seeking solutions to some of their numerous problems. The way I try to go about this assignment is that I try to be as elastic as possible. When poetry and prose did not work, I turned to mainstream drama. When I found out that that could not work because I needed a theatre house for that purpose and could not find any one to construct one, I turned to Theatre for Development (People Theatre) where you take theatre to the people, rather than the people to the theatre. And finding that initiative still not satisfactory, I am turning to cinema (People Cinema). So I am always searching for new ways of getting the message of hope rather than despair, of pro-action rather than fatalism, to the common people.

E. N. Ngwang: What in particular do you see or perceive to be your role as a leading Cameroonian dramatist, and how successful do you think you have been in executing this grave responsibility? Quantitatively and qualitatively, you have written more plays than any other Cameroonian dramatist that I know.

Prof. Butake: I don't know if I am a leading Cameroonian dramatist or whether I have a particular role to play other than that of a university teacher and someone who through his creative work seems to be concerned with the well-being of the Cameroonian masses. I grew up in very difficult circumstances and I have a very strong conscience which keeps steering me away from taking decisions that are likely to hurt others and my conscience. I am not particularly attracted to the acquisition of wealth by every means possible. So there are things that I react to practically instinctively especially where my conscience is going to be affected. I do not object to certain government policies because I want to play to the gallery, but rather because I analyze them and come to the conclusion that they will hurt the majority of Cameroonians and please the same few who have become veritable vampires.

I do not know how far I have succeeded in this grave responsibility; but I am very happy when I go back to primary schools in Bamendank-we, Awing, Benakuma, Nkor, or Binka (all villages in the Northwest Province of Cameroon) where I previously did workshops on environmental protection and discover that the schools now have orchards and premises blooming with flowers. Or I show up in Nkambe or Ndu in the North-West Cameroon and a Mbororo man comes up to me to say hello and mention the wonderful work I did with their women by encouraging them, through theatre, to break out of their cocoons and the culture of silence which had entrapped and imprisoned their lives for so long. Perhaps these examples are a measurement of the extent of my achievement in my role as a playwright.

E. N. Ngwang: You have just raised the issue of your background, that is, growing up in very difficult circumstances, which I very well know and share with you. How did these circumstances shape you as a playwright and would I be accurate to say some, if not all of your plays, are highly autobiographical? If any, which of your plays draw on the circumstances of your upbringing?

Prof. Butake: The difficult circumstances of my childhood arose from the fact that I lost both of my parents in the same week when I was barely four years old. My twin sisters who were barely three months old were taken to the orphanage in Shisong, Bui Division where they also died a few months later. I do not know the circumstances that led either to the deaths of my parents or my twin sisters. I was still too young to understand any of those things. So going through primary school and secondary school especially was very traumatizing for me because of the problem of school fees. I lived perpetually under the fear of being sent out of school for fees. I never had the luxuries of having new and fashionable stuff. As far as the plays go, there may be unconscious references to some autobiographical incidents but these are really only accidental. So, no, my plays are not autobiographical *senso stricto*.

E. N. Ngwang: Of all the plays you have written, which of them would you consider your best, your most representative, play and why?

Prof. Butake: That is a rather difficult question for me. It depends on the mood in which I find myself. Sometimes I think that *Lake God* is my best because of the poetry and the very deep emotional engagement. Another time it is *And Palm Wine Will Flow* because of the poetry and the great rapidity of action and the tightness of the plot. Again, it might be *Shoes and Four Men in Arms* or *Dance of the Vampires* because of the themes of totalitarianism, repression and popular uprising. It depends on how I am feeling at that particular moment of composition and the circumstances of my speculation about the plays or the societal atmosphere at the moment of thinking.

E. N. Ngwang: The peak of your writing career seems to fall within the period of great political upheavals and uprisings in Cameroon, especially the time when political pluralism was reintroduced into the political life of Cameroon. To what extent do your plays reflect this unrest or are we overshooting the mark if we were to consider your plays as political protest drama? And what are you protesting against and for?

Prof. Butake: While it is probably true that some of my plays were inspired by the political events of the 1990s, seeing that no artist creates in a vacuum, I would doubt that I have already gone past the peak of my creative work since I am still alive and still creating. It is not possible for me to interpret my works. It is left for the critic to do that. The fact that some of the plays were inspired by the events of that period is, perhaps, a good starting point for the critic. But if we tie down the works to a one-to-one interpretation, we might be overshooting the mark, considering that we cannot say what is likely to happen in future and whether future generations of readers will find any relevance in these plays to the events of their time. As for the protest aspect, it is clear that my creative work constitutes protest against injustice, cheating, corruption, repression, deprivation, immorality, lack of vision, etc.

E. N. Ngwang: There have been recent calls by English-speaking Cameroonians for total independence from what they term re-colonization of the British Southern Cameroons (formerly West Cameroon) by French (East) Cameroon. This has led to the formation of political lobby and pressure groups among which are the Southern Cameroons National Council (SCNC) now known as the British Southern Cameroons Nation (BSC Nation), the Cameroon Anglophone Movement (CAM), etc. What is your position in and take on these mushrooming pressure groups? And as an Anglophone yourself, have you been able to address their plight in any of your works?

Prof. Butake: Injustice, cheating, corruption, immorality, deprivation, tribalism, nepotism, neo-colonialism, etcetera, know no discrimination. The injustices suffered by Anglophones are unique and glaring only because there was an agreement between two parties at the moment of reunification that both groups (the Anglophones and Francophones) would relate as equals to form a federation of two states, with each respecting the other's sociocultural, legal, and political values, which sometimes are radically opposed to each other. Moreover, Anglophones seem to be more awake to questions of right and wrong, democracy, and the absence of it than the Francophones. Consider for a minute the persecution being visited upon the Baka (Pygmies) of the Equatorial Forests in the South and East Provinces. Are they any better than Anglophones because they are Francophones? Our problem in Cameroon today is that the political leadership is completely devoid of a social program for the Cameroonian people. Is it possible to have a country in which those in power regard dialogue with its own people as a show of weakness? In Cameroon dialogue or democracy has been replaced by the *baton de commandement*,[3] resulting in refusal to organize free and fair elections, the unleashing of the armed forces against a population that is struggling to survive with its bare hands.

So I agree with Anglophones that there has been a breach of agreement and confidence and treaties, etc. Will the British help? Very doubtful, seeing that they are brothers to the French who are controlling our leaders. Above all, the so-called leaders of the numerous Anglophone organizations are faring no better. Each one is struggling for influence and to attain to a position of power. Nothing will work in the present state of affairs. I was an original member of the SCNC and my name was even published by *Jeune Afrique Economie* as one of the Anglophone terrorists. I strongly believe that these movements or pressure groups need serious re-structuring and serious re-thinking of their strategies for any goals to be achievable. There are too many factions; which is why the neo-colonialist government does not care. The same fate has visited the opposition in Cameroon which is seriously in factions and cannot forge a unified front in order to confront the decadent oligarchy in power.

The example of the recent elections in Kenya should ring a bell in the ears of those who care to listen. The Anglophone problem will be solved the day all Cameroonians will decide to follow the example of the Kenyan people—fall behind one opposition leader for liberation.

E. N. Ngwang: As you look forward to the evolution on the political scene in Cameroon (the unhealthy relations between the Anglophones and the majority Francophones), what do you predict lies ahead? And does this future present challenges to you as a playwright, the conscience of the people?

Prof. Butake: I think I have already given the answer to this question above. Suffice it for me to say in addition that, as an artist, a playwright, I know that every story has a beginning, a middle, and an end. We have long gone past the middle of the story of the present regime in Cameroon.

E. N. Ngwang: In one of my articles on your works (accepted for publication in *The Literary Griot*), I compared you to the Kenyan, Ngugi wa

Thiong'o, in terms of your dedication to the plight of the local people in a fast changing environment. I will send the paper to you by attachment so that you can have a better understanding of the context of this analogy. Was this an accurate assessment of your role as a playwright, and do you face the same or similar problems Ngugi faced in Kenya? If not, how and in what ways is your situation different from Ngugi's?

Prof. Butake: Like every creative artist, I have been influenced by other writers. I admire Chinua Achebe for his manipulation of language, Ngugi for his concern for the marginalized masses, Soyinka for his plots, Athol Fugard for characterization, etc. But, of course, my major preoccupation in my works is with the predicament of the masses, especially their inability to grapple with poverty and ignorance. In addition, I know that Ngugi had problems with the ultra-conservative rulers of Kenya and was thrown into jail and later went into exile. My situation is different because I am not confrontational in my approach. I usually present things in such a way that those in authority see some good just as the deprived do, too. A teacher, without any pretensions of professionalism, does not tell his/her students that they are stupid or dull or ignorant. That is what I try to do for both parties. And this has spared me the torture and extreme persecution Ngugi was subjected to in Kenya. However, I have had my own shares of persecution, albeit small compared to others.

E. N. Ngwang: I know you are a full professor at the University of Yaoundé 1. How do you joggle between being a professor, playwright, visiting lecturer, and director of the university troupe? I remember working with you on Eugene O Neill's *The Emperor Jones* and some American plays when I was with you at the University of Yaoundé 1. What specific problems have you faced assuming these multiple roles in and out of the University and Cameroon? By the way, let me congratulate you on your promotion to the rank of Professor, which came after I had left the University of Yaoundé 1.

Prof. Butake: It is a matter of planning. In the theatre, the very first lesson you must learn is discipline. No one who is undisciplined can function well in the theatre. I generally plan my field trips to fall during the vacation period or I do catch-up lectures either before I depart on or upon my return from my trip. As for the university troupe, I have a number of younger colleagues who do most of the work. However, the lack of a performance space and funding from the university has resulted in a drastic reduction in productions. It is a matter of planning. And when I do have a trip abroad, I use it for writing.

E. N. Ngwang: In response to one of my previous questions, you asserted that you dropped poetry and the short story for drama because of "low readership" and somewhere you maintained that your target audience is the rural communities. Yet, most of your themes are urban, that is, they deal with issues of modern city life such as corruption, dictatorship, and political power. In a society where the rural population is far removed from the arena of these problems, how did you conceive to effect the desired change through your writing? Moreover, your basic language of communication here is Standard English. Have you considered using either Pidgin English or any of the local languages in order to reach a broader audience?

Prof. Butake: What I am saying is that I have found written plays inadequate for the purposes of conscientization because the plays are performed very rarely due to a lack of a traditional theatre hall where spectators can watch the plays and those of others on a more or less permanent basis. That is why I have moved on to People Theatre where, in a workshop situation with village participants, together we research into a specific problem, such as their water supply maintenance or HIV-AIDS or women's rights or human rights and democracy, or minority rights of the Baka (Pygmies), etc. We then create a story using the techniques of participation and improvisation, in the language that they are most comfortable with. This story is then rehearsed and performed in some public space in the village such as the market square, the chief's palace, the Church yard or the school compound. Some open space where people gather easily and quickly is transformed into an arena for acting.

And because our story or play deals with issues that they can recognize as theirs, because it is played by people whom they know and in their own language or a language that they have no difficulty following (such as Pidgin English), because they also have the opportunity to participate in the post-performance discussion at the end of the show, there is no doubt that they go back to their homes with some clear ideas and pride because they can see their problems, language, idioms, songs, and dances, etc. being given value, being brought to life. We use a similar technique in People Cinema, the only difference being that the story is now filmed professionally by a technical team from Cameroon Radio Television (CRTV), edited, mixed, and then screened for a much wider audience than the few hundreds or thousands who watch our performances in the villages or urban slums. That is why my focus is shifting away from mainstream drama to popular culture.

E. N. Ngwang: You also make allusions to women, especially to the reactions of Mbororo men and their women. Indeed, women play a very crucial role in most of your plays: Mboysi in *The Survivor* and the Wives in *Lake God* and *And Palm Wine Will Flow* . . . etc. What role do you conceive women will play in the new political dispensation in Cameroon, and do you think they can offer to the society what our men have failed to deliver? (i.e., in *The Survivor*, Mboysi is the ray of hope, in *And Palm Wine Will Flow*, it is the women under the leadership of Kwengong who unseat the Fon and institute a democratic system of governance). Do you foresee a new dawn for women on the political scene in Cameroon where women will be the main actors rather than merely appendages of their husbands or men?

Prof. Butake: Personally, I have a lot of hope in our womenfolk, especially when I see the very crucial economic role they play in every home. Women are the best managers in Cameroon and maybe elsewhere, too. However, when I observe the young women in our universities, the majority make my heart ache. They are mostly butterflies fluttering after wealth and not taking life seriously. When you look at the political parties in Cameroon, the women are not really making any inroads. Above all, it is unfortunate that the political impasse in which Cameroon finds itself today could really be diffused by women if only they could take up their political responsibilities as seriously as they take the responsibility of taking care of their families. When it comes to the political game most of our women become mere pawns in the hands of the men who manipulate them at will. This is a very tragic situation for Cameroon.

Many NGOs have been engaged in the training of women to take a more proactive role in the political sphere of Cameroon, but there is not much improvement. It is really difficult for me to reconcile this laissez-faire attitude with the great economic and managerial prowess and potential women exhibit in their homes. My sincere hope is that our women would soon realize that the political predicament of Cameroon rests in their hands. I am anxiously waiting for them to come to that realization and save the country from total disintegration.

E. N. Ngwang: In opposition to the very politically astute women of your rural plays, you have depicted the urban women in *The Rape of Michelle* as apolitical and corrupt. Rufina is the direct antithesis of Kwengong and the women that form the Chorus in *Lake God* and *And Palm Wine Will Flow*. Is the urban woman as corrupt as the men, or is she merely a victim of a brutal system that would corrupt the best in women? There is fear that once the Kwengongs visit the city they will lose their moral fiber. Or, put in another way, will the villages become also corrupt if they are urbanized? If so, what hope do we have for the country that will inevitably become urbanized someday?

Prof. Butake: There are very few educated urban women in Cameroon who would buy a newspaper to read or listen to the radio or watch television for any other reason other than for entertainment. Most of them are not interested in political developments. And so they have abandoned the playground to the urban illiterate woman who is easily manipulated by the corrupt politicians. Our educated women need to become more interested in politics in order to pull their somewhat ignorant sisters along.

E. N. Ngwang: Some time ago (I cannot recollect the exact date) you were quoted in *Cameroon Tribune* as having turned down an invitation by the ruling Cameroon People's Democratic Movement (CPDM) Party to go to your division on its political campaign team. In fact, you said you did not want to be "Lapiroed." Do you remember this date and why you turned down this invitation? How did the [CDPM] party receive it? Did you suffer any repercussions from this act of unprecedented effrontery and bravery? Why did you coin this word "Lapiroed?" I find this metaphor to be very germane to the circumstances that surrounded the political fate of artists in Cameroon; who was Lapiro and what was his fate?

Prof. Butake: In the late 1980s and more especially during the tumultuous '90s of multi-party politics, Lapiro de Mbanga was a very popular musician whose satirical and scathing songs against government policies made him popular among ordinary people in the urban centers of Douala and Yaoundé. During the Ghost Towns campaigns (a total shutdown of business in all major cities, except on Saturdays and Sundays) launched by the Coalition of Opposition Parties to coerce Paul Biya into convening a Sovereign National Conference, apparently Lapiro de Mbanga was bribed by Fochivé, the Secret Police chief, to go to the radio and television stations and urge his admirers to abandon the Ghost Town affair, which he did. The consequences were terribly dramatic and tragic for Lapiro.[4] People who had bought his audiocassettes destroyed them and he was physically attacked and almost lynched by a crowd in Douala. His car was burnt. Lapiro de Mbanga's reputation went down the drain in the twinkle of an eye. Today, he is again tying to sing revolutionary songs but no one is listening. If he was a traitor once, he could be again.

So when I was told that my name had been announced on national radio as chargé de missions for the CPDM party on a delegation to Kumba for the legislative elections of 1992, I immediately issued a disclaimer captioned, "I refuse to be Lapiroed" which was first published in *Cameroon Post* and then practically in all the other privately published newspapers in Cameroon in English and French. *Cameroon Tribune*, being a government newspaper, could never have published my disclaimer. I don't know how the party received it. But I know that one week after that disclaimer was published, Ngolle Ngolle was appointed a minister in my stead. After that, as far as I can remember, only one government functionary tried to persecute me. That was the chancellor of the university, Peter Agbor Tabi, who stopped all theatre performances in the university campus and all financial assistance to the performing arts. The situation has not changed today. My productions were crippled.

E. N. Ngwang: As I look back at your commitment to political satire and the danger to which you exposed your life, I see that many of your international predecessors opted for exile instead of taking the bull by the horns (to use a cliché). The Irish James Joyce in *A Portrait of the Artist as a Young Man* said he would not serve what he did no longer believe in and opted for exile, Samuel Beckett of the same nationality did the same, Soyinka had done the same. Have you ever considered exile as another alternative? Your voice seems to be the lone dramatic voice clamoring for the redress or political change. Or are there other Cameroonian dramatists engaged in the same war against the corrupt, dictatorial, and tribalized/tribalistic, and irredeemable regime that lords over Cameroonians?

Prof. Butake: In fact, there are a few people in Cameroon who would be very happy if I opted to go into exile. So far I haven't found any need to consider exile as an option. In fact, I doubt that I would be a happy person were I obliged to go into exile. I sincerely hope that the situation never arises because I love my country immensely.

Bate Besong,[5] playwright, poet and critic, is very critical of the problems faced by Anglophones in Cameroon; he has suffered detention in police custody because of his plays. There are a few others. But the difference is that I am a public figure because I participate in both radio and television programs on a very constant basis. The more public you become the more protected from outright persecution you are, because the government knows it will be held responsible for your demise.

E. N. Ngwang: Have you considered running for political office, to become a parliamentarian or deputy in order to use such an office as a platform for political change at the national level? Presently, the effect of your plays and audience seem to be limited to local areas where you have had workshops or where the plays have been taught in some classrooms.

Prof. Butake: I cannot run for political office on the ticket of any political party because politics deals chiefly in falsehoods and I don't know how to tell lies or how to play the dirty political game. But I am, and will always be, in the opposition no matter whichever party is in power. I believe it is the right stance for me as a creative writer. It is unfortunate for me that I cannot hide in Cameroon. It is very difficult for me to go somewhere in Cameroon and not be recognized by someone. Sometimes, it is quite embarrassing for me because I have to rack my mind trying to remember to no avail where I met the persons who greeted me with such familiarity. Such popularity fades easily when, as a politician or parliamentarian, you cannot deliver the goods to your people.

E. N. Ngwang: Considering the fact that your themes are political and the plays address contemporary political malaise in Cameroon, would you quit writing plays were these issues resolved magically overnight? Also looking back at the corpus of plays you have written and produced and some of the changes that have taken place on the political scene in Cameroon—hypothetically, if you had to re-write some of your plays, what would you change (add or expunge) in them, and which of your plays will be most affected?

Prof. Butake: There are a lot of other themes that I would be dealing with were the political issues resolved today. In addition, there is nothing that I would take out from any of the already written plays because there is always some relevance in them for somewhere. I do not believe in revising completed works which already have an existence of their own. I prefer to go ahead and do something else, for they addressed the issues that existed when they were written. They will remain as part of history, and as a reminder of the past and a guide to the future.

E. N. Ngwang: I consider appetite either in the form of eating or drinking as a central metaphor in your drama (the maggot in *The Survivor*, the vampire in *Dance of the Vampire,* palm wine in *Lake God* and *And Palm Wine Will Flow,* wine and food in *The Rape of Michelle*, etc.) which conjures images of disgust and this pits you squarely with Ayi Kwei Armah in *The Beautyful Ones Are Not Yet Born* (1968). Why this particular attraction to gastronomic imagery?

Prof. Butake: Because, unfortunately, the people do not have any other type of entertainment apart from football, drinking, dancing, and sex. There is the common saying in Cameroon that our politics is the politics of the belly—which may explain why people appointed to positions suddenly grow fat and clumsy and that every political gathering always ends with the leaders eating and drinking of supplies contributed by the poor political militants who themselves do not even eat the food or participate in the feasting.

E. N. Ngwang: As a prominent playwright in Cameroon and as your plays are becoming very popular and being taught all over the world and translated into other world languages, I assume you are continuously engaged in writing or thinking about new plays. What plays are you working on now? Can you tell us how and when your next play will come out, and what can we expect from you this time around?

Prof. Butake: I have many projects some of which might never see the light of day unless God gives me good health, energy, peace of mind, and a few more years to live. However, I never count my chicks until they are hatched. But I am working hard, very hard even.

E. N. Ngwang: Professor Butake, I thank you very much for your precious time. I am pleased to have been your undergraduate student and to look back at all those years at the University of Yaoundé 1 where and when you taught me African Literature. I look forward to reading and teaching your next play. In fact, I have taught most of the plays in *Lake God and Other Plays* to my college students, and they love them. It's been a remarkable pleasure interviewing you via the Internet. May the Lord bless and prosper you in your effort to make the world know Cameroon better and intimately.

Professor Bole Butake: The pleasure has been mine. I am also proud of your achievements, which go to show that we did a remarkable job molding you into a scholar. Good-bye.

Emmanuel N. Ngwang: Good-bye. I look forward to reading more works from you, especially those you are working on now.

NOTES

1. Interviewed on the Internet. This interview took place in the summer of 2003, and much has happened in Cameroon since. There have been subtle changes in the political setup and in government attempts to fight corruption and embezzlement, which resulted in the arrest and incarceration of some top government employees and ministers. Some were brought to trial while others were not, but the underlying perception and reception of this strategic initiative was that some of those arrested were those who challenged the ruling government over ineptitude. After all, it is the same political party and president who have been ruling Cameroon since 1982.

2. RDPC (Rassemblement Démocratique du Peuple Camerounais) is the French acronym for the Cameroon People's Democratic Movement (CPDM), the ruling political party headed by President Paul Biya, who doubles as chair of the ruling party and president of the country.

3. *Baton de commandement* is a French phrase translated as "a rod or baton of Command," used to signify the passing down of political power to a successor or appointed successor as opposed to the handing over of power through elections or popular votes.

4. The interview took place in 2003 when Lapiro de Mbanga was still alive. Unfortunately, he died recently on March 16, 2014, in Buffalo, New York, after a protracted illness.

5. Of greater artistic significance was the untimely passing of Dr. Bate Besong in a fatal car accident on his way from Buea to Yaoundé on March 8, 2007. May his soul rest in peace! He was one of the spirited Cameroon Anglophone dramatists and poets whose fiery satires constituted some of the most bitter and brazen attacks on the ruling political party.

THREE

The Political Dimensions of *Lake God and Other Plays*

Students of contemporary Cameroonian political history will immediately be struck by the similarities that exist between Bole Butake's satiric presentation of the abuse of political power, misuse of authority, and corruption that characterize the local communities of his plays and the current political dispensations in the Cameroonian society of the twenty-first century. Butake's collection of plays, written between 1982 and 1996, depict a society struggling under the iron grasp of corruption, nepotism and tribalism, the misuse and abuse of political power, and the attendant ills of dictatorship.

There is definitely a clear analogy between Butake's fictional world and the Cameroonian political system, the latter which provides Butake's plays with charged political undertones. In fact, these plays respond to specific events that took place in Cameroon in the 1980s and 1990s and which provided authentic occasions for the regime in power at the time to flex its muscles against the people it was set up to protect. Butake thus uses his plays to indict a regime that has outlived its usefulness, and by so doing, the playwright predicates his work on politics. In other words, Butake is a political playwright, pure and simple. Butake's restless social conscience is a reflection of the political restlessness inherent in his society. His plays are, in fact, the barometer of his audience, measuring through his own sense of the political observations the pressures and the political turmoil of the early 1990s. When conscripted to go on political campaign for President Biya's Cameroon People's Democratic Movement (CPDM) in the early 1990s, Butake declined saying he did not want to be "Lapiroed."[1] Like James Joyce's Stephen Dedalus in *A Portrait of the Artist as a Young Man*, Butake was no longer ready to serve a system or political setup in which he no longer believed.[2] Butake's refusal to participate in the campaign foreshadows Shey Ngong's refusal to obey the Fon in *And Palm Wine Will Flow*.[3] At this stage in his life, Butake met the Cameroonian established dictatorship head-on and won a tactical victory.

In order to comprehend Butake's plays, it is necessary for us to establish the global significance of the role of the writer in his society, one that moved from mere entertainment and information to political activism and conscientization as stated by Butake in Chapter One, the Interview. Unlike John Osborne in *Look Back in Anger*,[4] whose main character Jimmy Porter declares that there are no longer any causes or crusades worth fighting for, Butake approached the stage with a lot of optimism that where there is life, there is always hope. He embraced the club of other literary writers who came to grips with their responsibilities in the ongoing struggle against the ills of society.

If we examine the African literature of the immediate postcolonial period, we discern that it did not take long after independence for avowedly radical African writers to realize that something had gone terribly wrong. The Africans had experienced and envisioned decolonization as a time of massive political and socioeconomic transformation. Yet, looking around them at the aftermath, they quickly perceived that the so-called "revolution" had been derailed. The liberation that they had celebrated at independence was merely a deception and limited in its effects. It was, in fact, liberation to suit the narrow class interests the liberation leaders had initially deplored in the colonizers. There could be no peace, no tranquility in the face of the continued squalor, tribalism, sectionalism, dictatorship, and the tyranny that loomed ugly over most African nations. Most African nations quickly realized the savage irony of their situation. African writers then took upon themselves the awesome task of depicting the bleak vision of a continent that had suddenly been transformed from being ruled by colonial authorities to one ruled by Africans themselves. In most of the literature of the 1960s, the African writers tended to focus on the parasitism of the new African political class. Members of this class were exposed in their ruthlessness and vulgarity: there was their ethic of conspicuous consumption, their corruption, their greed and reckless materialism and, above all, there was the atrocious lack of vision.

This new political class was portrayed as "a murderously hypocritical social fraction, living not only beyond its own means but beyond the means of society as a whole."[5] This class of leaders constituted a kleptocracy ruling over countries and societies replete with continuing poverty and powerlessness of the peasants and local people toiling below them. Consequently, the decades following independence were characterized by social violence generated both by the rulers against their people, on the one hand, or the uprising of the people against continued exploitation, depredation and the intensifying structural dependence of Africa upon the imperial Western powers, who indirectly imposed the corrupt leaders on the citizenry.

The general point of agreement among the Anglophone writers of the 1960s was that the promised freedom and liberty fought for and which culminated in independence had failed or was subverted. Political critics like Franz Fanon and Aimé Cesare and artists (novelists, poets, and dramatists alike) began to be preoccupied with questions such as "What had gone wrong? Why? How had the revolution been subverted?" Betrayal became a central theme of most of the writing of this period. It is this radical introspection that culminated in the rise of the African protest novels and plays.

This relationship between the writer and his or her society was not only limited to Africa given the political situation of the world, the relations between the writer and society, between art and life, but it suggested a definite need for careful explorations and reappraisals. In his Prefatory Note to *The Politics of Twentieth-Century Novelists* (1974), George A. Panichas reevaluated these relationships.[6] In his opinion, the question about literature, which had limited itself to that of form and language, started giving way to a deeper evaluation of subject matter in response to the changing political scene. In early 1949, Mark Schorer issued a timely warning that the novel (and by extension the play), because of its intrinsic nature as an art form, necessarily opened itself to the "first question about philosophy . . . politics, and conduct,"[7] thereby shifting the center of literary aesthetic from form to subject.

In fact, by the mid-1940s, a second generation of critics began to rebel against the puritan rigidity and narrowness of the formalist approach of literature and sought to establish a critical perspective broad enough to include reader response, authorial intention, and ultimately the areas of philosophy, politics, and conduct which earlier critics were unwilling to explore. The principal effort of modern criticism became a substitution of an aesthetic reading for an older view of fiction as realistic documentation or propaganda: the idea that fiction should be read with the primary regard for the social and political views of the author. Literary paradigms started shifting from pure entertainment and pastime to some healthily realistic relationship of the life that provides its raw materials, with the artful presentation of that life appearing as an inescapable first consideration of any of its criticism.

Therefore, this shift in paradigm called for the reevaluation of the role of the artist in the society. The writer, insofar as he or she is an artist and something more than a social historian, is compelled in his or her intimate, practical relationship with his or her materials to work with specifics, with the single dramatic instances and concrete particulars of the experience he or she wishes to represent. So long as the writer believes that he or she is the chief custodian of sanity and civilization, his or her primary responsibility will be to criticize society for failing to be civilized and sane. He or she will inevitably ground his or her work on the state of politics or the condition of society. The writer cannot avoid this responsibility because he or she is part and parcel of that true and human world of which he or she is a living part: he or she is bound inevitably by cultural ties to speak the language of his or her audience. To the artist, literature is no longer a mere narrative of the age, but an invitation to action against what is wrong with his or her society, rebellion against all forms of abuses among which are hypocrisy, tyranny and dictatorship, kleptomania and kleptocracy, and corruption. As such, what and how the artist writer interweaves with the society in which he or she lives, the people he or she observes, and the civilization and conduct that comprise that society constitute the raw materials and vision to which he or she constantly returns for inspiration. The writer, therefore, helps in what Panichas refers to as "the normative consciousness of life," (xviii) which addresses itself to the overarching question of how humans live.

Increasingly, the modern writer is unable to separate himself/herself from the moral and political events of his or her time. He or she establishes a historical contact among the people who are steeped in the same history and who likewise contribute to making this history the target of the writer's conscious sense of commitment. It is equally an awareness of one's literary contribution as in itself an involvement in the problems and disasters of the age, as well as an awareness that the written work is an essential condition of action, that is, the moment of reflective consciousness. For the modern writer, politics in all its forms, as theory, as commitment, as action, has become a matter of consciousness and of conscience. The writer is indeed a creator who makes others act, transforming human destiny primarily into one of action. He or she is a protestant, a partisan whose central themes are resistance, rebellion, and death aimed at imposing on his or her society a vision of life that seems desirable.

Consequently, the modern artist has come to perceive his or her role not merely as one of entertainment but rather as one of the expression of meaning, the communication of insight into some aspect of reality and human experience, the questioning and redefining of values—a recorder and giver of social history. It is the artist's sense of responsibility and his or her commitment that informs and defines his or her role in society and in the creative process. The Italian novelist and politician Ignazio Silone saw this role clearly when he asserted that, "For me, writing has not been, and never could be, except in a few favored moments of grace, serene aesthetic enjoyment, but rather the painful and lonely continuation of a struggle."[8]

It is this same spirit, this same struggle to come to terms with reality, the truth, the ills of the society that goaded Butake to embrace social realism as his mode of dramaturgical rendition of his society. Although Butake's plays are set in a small rural community in the North West Region of Cameroon, the village is a microcosm of the entire nation, and the reaction of the authorities to the existing situation is a reflection of how the entire country is ruled. The plays deal with the corruption, tyranny, and the abuse of political power, issues of democracy, and human rights in contemporary African societies, especially in Cameroon. They are, in fact, an indictment of postcolonial regimes (and the case of Cameroon Biya's regime), which have become "dreams deferred," broken promises, promises made, and promises not kept.

Like a Fon in the Grassfields of Cameroon, Biya's coming to power in Cameroon was greeted with a lot of euphoria and jubilation by the citizens, who saw in his coming to power promises of reconciliation, hope, justice for all and a new face-lift for those tribes and regions that were formerly ignored and/or persecuted by Biya's predecessor Ahmadou Ahidjo. Initially, Biya was highly praised for his early reformist inclinations. Takougang and Krieger's insightful depiction of the early days of Biya's rule reveals the euphoria with which Biya was greeted.[9] Biya's maiden tours round the country and his speeches promised a new dawn for Cameroonian politics, one built on freedoms and western-style democracy. No sooner did Biya obtain political power than he turned round and disappointed the citizens he had promised to serve faithfully. His New Deal philosophy became simply rhetoric, and tribalism and favoritism became his watchwords. In *And Palm Wine Will Flow,* the Fon's greatest supporter turned greatest critic, Shey Ngong, complains that, "I am no dog that will hunt for the pleasure of another. . . . But your Fon knows none other than his family and those that come to him with gifts in return for the red feather" (91). This indeed is a reflection of what became of the New Deal philosophy after Biya consolidated his hold on Cameroon.

The Fon has degenerated from the position of protector of the people's land to one who "pronounces that this farmland belongs to himself or one of his family." He is now "the pig who knows only the hunger of its own stomach" (91), and surrounded, not by wise king makers and elders, but by "his family of hand-clappers." This reminds us of Shakespeare's Macbeth, who regrets that at his old age he is surrounded by flatterers and people who fear for their life:

> This push
> Will cheer me ever, or disseat me now,
> I have liv'd long enough. My way of life
> Is fallen into the sear, the yellow leaf;
> And that which should accompany old age,
> As honour, love, obedience, troops of friends,
> I must not look to have; but in their stead,
> Curses, not loud but deep, mouth-honour, breadth
> Which the poor heart would fain deny, and dare not.[10]

However, unlike Shakespeare's King who attains a certain degree of self-knowledge and still goes out to fight "bear-like," Butake's Fon meets his end still believing that power and justice are on his side. Thus, he threatens Kwengong saying:

Watch your tongue, woman! Earth-goddess indeed!
Your wretched husband, the self-made priest of
Nonexistent gods and sower of bad words against
Our royal person, is still too smart from the venom of my power
And you dare to insult our royal presence
By profanely pronouncing our sacred name? (109)

Kwengong's response to the Fon implies that the Fon lost his sacred name the day he ignored the tradition that put him on the throne. The royal or political power has reverted to the people:

The only husband Earth-goddess honours, Chila Kintasi,
Is the whole land of Ewawa,
Here are the fruits [the women] urged me feed the crocodile that swal-
lows its own eggs! (110)

Here, the hunter has become the hunted. The image of the crocodile here is very appropriate because the crocodile is supposed to protect its eggs jealously; rather, it feeds on them. The Fon has betrayed the trust of the villagers whom he was supposed to protect; he has turned against them. As a kind of punishment, Kwengong forces the Fon to drink the urine "from the vaginas of those upon whom [he] wields power . . . / And feel the power of power" (110). In fact, in Ewawa village, like in other African villages, the magical power of the women is incontestable. In the early 1990s, this was demonstrated in Bamenda by elderly women, the "Takumbeng," who marched naked to the District Office to demand the release of their husbands. Butake, in fact, recognizes the sacred powers of women in matters of grave importance when he depicts these women as the courageous force capable of effecting a permanent political change in Ewawa. The Fon dies on drinking the women's urine. Indeed, it is Kwengong who has the last word in the play: "the women have decided. No more Fons in the land . . . the people will rule through the council of elders led by Shey, here" (113). The men come in only to execute the decisions taken by the women; they are energized and emboldened only by the women. This, indeed, is Butake's call for women to take a more active part in politics, especially as men have apparently become cowards. The dialogue between two nobles Shey Ngong and Nsangong reflects the contempt the nobles have for the Fon:

Shey Ngong: Another red feather? Only Kibanya was due to be honoured today. When this land was still the land empty shells like Kibanya would never have had access to the palace. Today, nobles have become slaves and slaves nobles. Just because the late Fon . . .
Nsangong: When there is too much in the belly, the head becomes an empty shell . . . (92–93)

The Fon has not only become a usurper, but he has equally lost his sanity. He has become the proverbial "empty shell," propped on the shoulders of "slaves" (the good-for-nothings) who inadvertently have become the nobles. Unlike in Shakespeare's *Macbeth* where Macbeth himself regrets a similar unfortunate turn of events, Butake's Fon takes delight in mediocrity. He keeps company with "manless men like Kibanya [who] have their caps topped with the red feather by the Fon himself" (96). The retribution for dishonoring the Fon is the loss of landed property. The Tapper tells Shey Ngong:

> The Fon has seized the palm-bush. His watch-dogs are there now. Getting drunk on the wine I tapped. Look at my clothes! All torn! All tatters!
>
> Shey, they beat me up severely. . . . They were already drunk. They had finished a whole pot of wine which I tapped yesterday. When I asked them what they wanted, they laughed and said the palm-bush had reverted to the Fon, its rightful owner. The Fon is mad. (98–99)

Earlier, Nsangong had informed Shey Ngong, the activist, that his (i.e., Ngong's) wives' lands have been seized and given to Kibanya's wives, and that the Fon's stooges were rejoicing in Shey Ngong's misfortune (92–92). Kwengong, one of the elders, brings Shey Ngong more bad news:

> The times are changing, Shey. The times have changed. Look at you! What is your reward? After how many years of loyal service to the gods and the land? The farmlands of your wives have been given to the wives of the lowliest of the low. Why? Because he pays respect to the Fon. But you . . . (97)

Shey Ngong's response to this political move by the Fon reveals the extent to which traditional values have been abused and adulterated by the incompetent Fon:

> **Shey Ngong:** Wife, I will not pay respect to a man who respects only palm-wine and food. When does the Fon really rule? How often has he consulted the council of elders or even implemented decisions by that revered body for the common good of the all the land? (97)

Shey Ngong's disenchantment with the Fon emanates from the latter's diversion from the preconceived and inherited responsibility of the chief, which is one of catering for the common weal of the people, one determined by the council of elders, the modern political equivalence of the cabinet of ministers and the legislature. The revered cabinet has been replaced with a rubber-stamp assembly of hand clappers, "those clamoring for the red feather [and] only making the Fon richer. Today, with a few goats and fowls even the low are beginning to file into the royal presence. How do you have a land in which everyone is a title-holder?" (97). Shey Ngong then regrets "Where have our values of old gone? I spit on the distributer of the red feather." (98) In fact, Shey Ngong regrets having participated in the enthronement of the Fon, who has now turned against him: "If I had not insisted that he should be crowned . . . the elders would never have accepted . . . for as soon as he smelled, tasted and felt power, he turned against me" (106).

Shey Ngong's regret parallels the attitude and fate of Pa Foncha, the former prime minister of West Cameroon and later vice president of Cameroon who was frustrated and stripped of power by Paul Biya as soon as the latter consolidated his hold on Cameroon through the unpopular annexation of West Cameroon in the teleguided referendum of May 20, 1972, initiated by his predecessor, Ahmadou Ahidjo. The Federal Republic of Cameroon was reverted to the United Republic of Cameroon, and finally back to the Republic of Cameroon. Although Butake's plays do not refer obliquely to this maneuver, the spirit of frustration and disenchantment witnessed in the palace, especially in *And Palm Wine Will Flow*, reflects the same spirit that was evident among the Cameroonians of the English-speaking regions, the Bamilikes, and the other regions who had all hailed the coming of Biya to power. As in the play, Cameroon became a country of two worlds: the world of the inner circle of the powerful who dispose of the country's wealth and the world of the outsiders who looked dejectedly at the greedy insiders. In fact, the insiders have the impunity not only to abuse power, but also to misappropriate the citizens' property:

> The Tapper: The Fon has seized the palm bush. His watch-dogs are there now. They beat me severely. My clothes are all tatters. . . (107)

The Fon and his hand-clapping entourage spend their time, not thinking about and engaging in political discourse or initiatives for running the Fondom efficiently. Instead, they engage in drinking and rejoicing over the misfortune of the outsiders who have been stripped of their dignity. Shey Ngong confirms this unfortunate turn of events by saying rhetorically, "Naturally! Is there a single day in this land that they are not drinking? The sun cannot rise and set in this land without someone taking a title or some other celebration" (107). Shey Ngong's attitude is not one of envy or jealousy, but one of grave concern for a society where ancient values of hard work, respect, and clear thinking have been prostituted for loud-mouth praises and fame.

Butake's restless conscience propels him to a point of outright overthrow of the Fon. In fact, Butake does not subscribe to the idea that the Fon is invincible. Indeed, the trouble with the village is the Fon himself. Unlike in Sophocles' *Oedipus*, where Oedipus comes to the self-realization that he is responsible for the curse on the land and that the only solution or cure lies in his being purged out of the city he loves so much, Butake's Fon does not come to terms with his own weaknesses. After all, those who surround him are not intent on telling him his fault, but rather in condoning and protecting his weaknesses and reaping their own reward while the Fon stays in power. Kwengong, who assumes the leadership role of the women, confronts the Fon with the power of the people.

She is so bold as to confront the Fon about the latter's loss of authority. She believes that salvation will only come to the village after the death of the Fon. Hence, she tells the Fon,

> Then you will die indeed, Chila Kintasi,
> Your own mouth pronounced judgement.
> Die and deliver the land from the
> Abominations of drunkenness and gluttony
> Die! Chila Kintasi, die!
> And save the land from merry-making!
> Die Fon! So that we may think!
> The people need your death to think!
> Die! Die! Die! (110)

Tapper is emboldened by Kwengong's bravery to assert the need for action:

> Shey, it is time for action.
> None of his blood must be allowed to succeed.
> The palace must be burnt down.
> No more Fons in this land!
> They neither rule with the head nor with the heart.
> I say, no more fons. (110–11)

The citizens revert to the status quo, when they were ruled by "the council of elders led by the chief priest of Nyombom." Henceforth, "the people will decide who that will be and for how long. And the affairs of the land shall be decided by the people in the market place" (111). What Kwengong is advocating is the modern equivalence of a democracy—a government of the people decided upon by the people, and for the people. This government would owe its existence to the people and would be responsible to the people, the common people, who have the right and duty in deciding who rules over them and for how long. This will be a modern day functional National Assembly, which will replace the hand-clapping assemblies of the past.

Another dimension which Kwengong brings to the new form of government is that its term of office must be predetermined and limited. This new outlook runs contrary to the views of some African heads of state such as the late Emperor Jean Bedel Bokassa of Central African Republic who made themselves "presidents for life," or those who ruled as if they never had the intention of leaving office. If there were limitations placed on these governments, leaders would surely be conscious of rendering accounts of their stewardship to the people at the end of their terms. Their fear of the day of reckoning would have instilled in them the fear of retribution and accountability.

According to Kwengong, a new system of governance must be installed in the land for peace to return to the people. Henceforth,

> The people will be ruled through the council of elders led by Shey. . . .
> The day that he [Shey] takes a wrong decision, that same day, the
> people shall meet in the market place and put another at the head of
> the council of elders. (113)

Indeed, Butake is subtle enough to introduce the political influence and
prowess of women without suggesting the takeover of the traditional
leadership of men. The women do the background and foot work and
retreat to the background while pushing their husbands to the forefront.
This raises the questions as to if Butake envisioned that women were not
quite ready or prepared to take over total power from these failed men.
This indeed will be another topic of discussion. However, Shey Ngong
accepts the women's challenge and promises that "And the affairs of this
land shall be debated in the market place." To which Tapper adds, in a
way of confirmation, "No more secrets in the land." As Kwengong calls
for the bugle to be sounded for the people to assemble in the market-
place, Shey Ngong immediately discerns in this move a return to the
corrupt past, as the bugle was a symbol of power of the past. He immediately calls for a clean break from the past:

> No. Not the bugle. We must break clean from the past. Take the sacred
> gong of Nyombom; And let it resound in all the nooks and corners of
> the land. From today, this bugle will stay here in the sacred grove, a
> living symbol of our enslavement by the Fon and his notables. Take the
> sacred gong to the people and let its sound vibrate through their very
> souls, a symbol of their liberation. (113)

Tapper's song, which ends the play, is an eulogy about the death of
dictatorship, a return of "power to the people," a slogan usually chanted
by the Cameroonian opposition party, the Social Democratic Front (SDF):

> People of Ewawa!
> People of this land!
> As the sun rises at dawn
> So shall we meet
> In the market-place
> To decide on the destiny of this land
> No more shall we allow
> One person to rule our land for us!
> From this moment, palm-wine shall no longer flow
> In this land of Ewawa,
> It shall be used sparingly
> In libations to the gods and ancestors!
> In preparing medicinal herbs for the sick!
> People of Ewawa, have you all heard?
> Have you heard the pronouncement?
> The pronouncement of the Earth-goddess, Nyombom?
> Have you heard the pronouncement of the land?
> Chorus: We have heard o o o o! (114)

And Palm-Wine Will Flow ends with the overthrow of traditional dictatorship, the end of the rule of one man and the empowering of the people. Power has now reverted to the people who must decide who rules over them and for how long. The return of power to the people is tantamount to the return of sanity to the people and the "rule of the head and heart" rather than the former "rule of the belly." The new village, new because it has a right to that name now, will be free of enslavement, bribery, and corruption. It will now be a village in which titles (metals of valor) will be given to people on the basis of merit and hard work, irrespective of tribe, age, and origin. It will be one in which the people will speak with one voice and the traditional and curative value of palm-wine will be reinstalled.

The play *The Rape of Michelle* shifts the center of action from the village to the urban center, to a chicken parlor where Michelle and her mother compete for the love of the school teacher Mikindong. Rufina, Michelle's mother, runs a chicken parlor which inextricably serves a double purpose: it is a place where people come to drink and eat and at the same time a venue where Rufina attracts potential sexual clients. Because Mikindong will not fall for the coquettish antiques of Michelle and her mother, the former forces herself into his house and stages a rape scene. Mikindong is apprehended by the police and locked up for days without trial.

What stands out clearly in the play is not the issue of prostitution, which is equally important, but the legal system which collapses in the establishment of justice. This play portrays a city that is totally corrupt, one in which every legal agent uses his vantage position to enrich himself. Mikindong is incarcerated and only released or given a break on the strength of the bribe his attorney gives to the prison guard and the Registrar: "Cost me thirty thousand francs to the Registrar" (84).

Later when Mikindong alludes to the fake medical certificate Michelle presented as evidence of rape, the attorney says: "You know yourself that money can fetch anything. That certificate was bought" (85). Mikindong asserts therefore that he is suffering the fate of so many innocent people in a situation where the law has become a toy in the hands of a corrupt judicial system:

> You know yourself that the law is what it is. Many innocent people get convicted while criminals go scot-free. All I ask of you is to make contact with the presiding magistrate. I know he would like an envelope. My wife has promised to see him. (185)

Mikindong finally comes to term with and embraces what the prison guard calls "practical philosophy," practiced religiously by those into whose hands the system of justice has been entrusted. The corrupt policeman thus lectures Mikindong:

> Teacher, let me tell you something. Whether you did it or not does not
> really matter. If you do not make contacts, you are going to stay in
> prison for a good part of your only life. And what will happen to your
> beautiful wife and your work? She will become the woman of some
> powerful man. But with money . . . you can move mountains. (186)

While biblically mountains can be moved through prayer (Mark
11:22–24), in Butake's play mountains can only be moved through corruption and bribery. Mikindong's release from detention is not a sign of
victory or the triumph of justice over injustice, but a lease for him to
collect money to bribe the presiding magistrate. After all, the policeman
knows he can manipulate Mikindong into submission to corruption by
threatening to deprive him of what he loves most—his life, his work, and
wife.

At the end of the play, Mikindong has been released from jail on bail
and is celebrating his appointment to the post of principal of a college.
We are told that the magistrate has not passed judgement because the
judgement or verdict will be determined by the bribe he receives from
Mikindong. This explains why the magistrate is disgusted with the lavish
celebration of Mikindong's appointment: "With all this celebration and
the champagne popping all over, you think they can still put together
something reasonable?" (198).

Zende, the lawyer, assures the magistrate that he (the lawyer) "might
just have to remind him" (198). As they are about to leave Mikindong's
house, the magistrate reminds Mikindong about what is at stake:

> Mr. Mikindong, again I congratulate you most heartily. In fact, I do so
> from the bottom of my heart. That is not a job that one should lose by
> going to jail. (198)

The price tag on being a free man in order to assume the post of principal
will definitely have to be high. Zende, the lawyer, had hinted Mikindong
that he and the magistrate "are friends. I have been talking to him this
evening as we were driving here, and he might just accept half-a-million"
(199). As the play ends, Mikindong bewails this life of absolute corruption: "Oh God! What a life. . . . But why should a man suffer so much and
lose so much money even though he is innocent?" (199).

Mikindong's question is one of morality and conscience. It speaks to
and for a system that has no regard for justice. In fact, the machinery of
justice is in the hands of those who wield political power. We see a
system in which even the attorneys and the magistrates recognize that
corruption and bribery are the order of the day. It is therefore no accident
that in two consecutive years, Cameroon won the infamous title of being
the most corrupt country in the world.[11] Like in Butake's *And Palm-Wine
Will Flow*, Zende's call for a revolution at the end of the day is prophetic.
In response to Mikindong's rhetorical question, "but why should a man

suffer so much and lose so much money even though he is innocent?"
Zende, the attorney, says:

> That is the problem. Until a revolution takes place, we will continue to
> function through the telephone call from above and the envelope from
> below, as your friend, the policeman, put it. And, you know, now that
> you have been appointed principal he is expecting a sizeable envelope.
> He now knows that you have everything to lose. (199)

Zende simply confirms what the practical philosopher, the policeman,
had earlier said to Mikindong:

> Contacts. A telephone call from above to the magistrate! An envelope
> from below to the magistrate! And the deed is done. The case is closed
> or simply thrown out of court. Contacts! Oh yes! We must be practical
> and realistic. You think the magistrate eats truth? You think the prose-
> cutor eats truth? Nobody eats truth. But people need a drink now and
> again. They need money to do things. That is what I call practical
> philosophy. (186)

Since bribery and corruption have become so entrenched in the society, it
will take a revolution for justice to regain its place. Thus, Butake prescribes an uprising, a revolution to overthrow the system that is corrupt.
It is a system in which everybody, including the policeman, the magistrate, and even the attorney, has become an accomplice in the game of
corruption. The intellectual (the teacher) and the lawyer have all been
emasculated by an all-powerful corrupt magistrate who uses the judicial
system to enrich himself. This situation stands in direct opposition to
what President Paul Biya outlined in the final chapter of his book *Communal Liberalism*:

> This strong quest for liberty does not mean the promotion of laissez-
> faire.
>   While liberalism advocates the granting of various liberties to man,
> it also expects man to appeal constantly to his reason and morally to his
> conscience. This is because reason and conscience are the only true
> qualities of Man who is convinced that he can enjoy his liberty only if
> he is capable of countering any temptation of laissez-faire and an-
> archy. . . . I would, therefore, like to insist on the duty of reason and
> conscience incumbent on all Cameroonians. Reason and conscience,
> which totally embody our desire for moral rectitude, are the basis of
> our project to build a liberal and democratic society. [12]

Biya's concept of social equality grounded in human personality, freedom of thought, and democracy exists only in a form of empty rhetoric.
According to Takougang and Krieger (1998), it is Biya's inability or lack
of fortitude to implement these changes, that is, to implement this lofty
concept of a new Cameroon of social justice that accounts for "the disillu-
sionment and the increased demand for urgent political reforms which
up to now are slow, if any, in coming" (97).

The corruption and bribery found in the urban areas in *The Rape of Michelle* are contagious. Even the village of Ewawa, far removed from the urban center, manifests these traits in yet a more sophisticated way. In *Lake God,* the Christian Fon, who now combines ancestral authority and Western Christianity with the backing of Father Leo, betrays the trust vested in him. The Christian Fon becomes an accomplice in the destruction of the crops on which the villages thrive. His cattle and those of Dewa destroy the villagers' crops, and when Dewa is brought before the Fon, he tells the women that the Bororos (the cattle rearers) cannot go away because they belong to the land. According to the Fon, the law forbids expulsion of anybody, especially the Bororos who are now considered legal citizens, and that progress in the village is tied to cattle. He tells Dewa to pay two thousand Francs (2,000 Frs) to each woman whose crops have been destroyed by the cattle. In this regard, one would be satisfied that some kind of justice has been done albeit minimal. However, the Fon turns around and tells Dewa: "You go muf two cow fo you nyun puttam for me nyun. Woman cow wey get leke three year so dat small tam get belle. You don hear fine, fine?" (Translated: You go and remove two of your own cows and add to mine. These should be mature female cows three years old that are ready to reproduce or be pregnant. Have you understood well?)

This attitude, materialistic and immoral as it is, echoes the same type of corruption we have in the urban centers. The Fon, who is traditionally considered the protector and guarantor of the villagers' rights and justice, succumbs to corruption. He profits, like the administration and police officers in *The Survivors,* from the calamity of the helpless women. Shey Bo-Nyo, reacting to the Fon's attitude, reminds the villagers that the Fon came to the throne through bribery and corruption. In fact, he is not taken aback by the Fon's attitude, given that the Fon bribed his way to chieftaincy.

Thus, the Fon subverts tradition through corruption and bribery. Unlike his father who was the bulwark of cultural values, the new Christian Fon betrays tradition by letting "the land go[es] to the dog" (19). Finally, Shey Bo-Nyo predicts that the Fon will destroy the land and himself. The only solution to this unfortunate situation comes from women. Under the leadership of Yensi, the women call for unity and courage in defiance of their cowardly husbands. In the end, the women call for the overthrow of the Fon and the death of Father Leo. They bring out their sacred power—their refusal to provide food—to force their husbands into action.

In the ongoing fight against the abuse of power, corruption, bribery, and tyranny, Butake eulogizes the woman and lifts her from her so-called traditional role of secondary status, household chores, and subservience to that of leadership. In *The Survivor,* it is, in fact, Mboysi who prostitutes her body to save her surviving family. However, she shoots the officer who used his position to extort sexual favors from her in exchange of food and shelter which were donated to be distributed to the survivors at no cost. Pointing the gun at the officer, Mboysi realizes that she now has absolute power over him, and that she must now use that power to make a point:

> Keep crawling, officer. This is the moment of truth. The moment of your death and the moment of our liberation. . . . Keep crawling, you rotten maggot! Even if I die after killing you, I will be satisfied that I had my revenge. Now, this is the moment of truth—Man! Man! Come and see what a woman can do. All of you, come along and celebrate the victory of woman over the police officer:
> Come along, all of you and celebrate your liberation.
> The elephant has fallen!
> The elephant has fallen!
> The lion is no more. (84)

Although Mboysi is shot by another officer who suddenly appears on the scene, her victory over the first officer cannot be ignored. Her courage before death bears testimony to the role women can and should play in the total liberation of the village and, by extension, the country. In *And Palm-Wine Will Flow*, it is Kwengong, one of the wives of Shey Ngong, who leads the women and ultimately the entire village to victory against the Fon. She reiterates the transvaluation of values that has become characteristic of the village:

> The only men left in the land are the women. And they do not want any more Fons. Get the antidote ready (112)

And later she declares the revolution against the Fon:

> The women have decided. No more Fons in the land. . . . The people will rule through the council of elders led by Shey, here. The day that he takes the wrong decision, that same day, the people shall meet in the market place and put another at the head of the council of elders. (113)

The women's secret society, the Fibuen, replaces the Kwifon and the Kibaranko, the male sacred societies that have been sent on exile. Although the women overthrow the Fon, they still secretly reserve the pride of leadership and "rulership" to their men, an honor entrenched in the male-dominated culture of the local people. Furthermore, in *The Rape of Michelle*, it is Michelle's mother, Rufina, who has corrupted and bribed the magistrate to deny Mikindong bail and to keep him in prison for as long as possible. On the other hand, Akwen, Mikindong's wife, is the antidote to Rufina. It is she who now holds the destiny of her husband in her hands. This comes out clearly in the conversation with the policeman about her husband's comfort in prison:

> Policeman: Madam, I will not do you a favor for nothing. You think I am on duty alone? There are three others there. . . What you are giving me cannot even buy a bottle of red wine. . . It all depends on you,

madam, our treatment of your husband depends on you. You can even
bring him a blanket and a tiny mattress, if you wish . . . yes, everything
depends on you. (180)

Mikindong is given a little bit of freedom and comfort because Akwen
buys all of this with money. Akwen is able to get a date for her husband's
court "hearing" because she had to bribe the registrar and the magistrate.
Thus, she promises her husband, "Don't worry too much. God will show
the way. I will try and see the presiding magistrate. I can't lose a husband
only after six months of marriage" (182). This marriage is still fresh and
new and deserves to be jealously preserved and fought for. Time becomes a determinant of the urgency of action to resolve the incarceration,
which threatens the deprivation and eventual loss of conjugal bliss.

Akwen decides to take charge of raising money to corrupt the magistrate knowing fully well that she has to compete with Rufina whose fight
is to delay, if not prevent Mikindong's trial. In this regard, Butake intimates that Akwen understands the language of "practical philosophy"
more than her husband does. However, unlike in *The Survivors, Lake God*
and *And Palm Will Flow* where the women take the roles of revolutionary
liberators through sacrificial self-denial, Akwen's role here is that of surviving through or going with the wind, acquiescing to bribery and corruption as the way forward. If the language of the day is corruption,
Akwen, like Rufina, is willing to speak it, too. So Mikindong's ultimate
victory will not be determined by how well his legal counsel defends him
or presents his case, but by "the size of the envelope" (i.e. the amount of
bribe money) and the maneuvers Akwen has to make behind the scene.

In *The Survivor*, Mboysi's death is sacrificial. She is the martyr who
dies in the service of her people in her struggle to liberate the survivors.
In *The Rape of Michelle*, Akwen "dies" a symbolic death. She dies to conscience and morality in order to save her husband. But in the latter case,
the future is still bleak because the verdict is still pending. It may be
Butake eschews this method of liberation that simply imprisons one to a
state of moral indebtedness since such a method would nullify his primary stance against corruption in any form. It is only Mboysi's death that
reveals in vivid terms the grotesque image of exploitation and corruption
epitomized in the image of the maggot:

> You will kill me, would you? You crawling, thieving maggot. Growing
> rich on the misfortune of others—Stuffing your decaying stomach and
> your bulging pockets on the calamity of my people. Never again shall
> you live to perpetuate our misery (83)

Mboysi's "never again" in *The Survivors* is reiterated in the same strong
terms by Kwengong in *And Palm-Wine Will Flow* when she says "No more
Fons in the land!" (113) and Tapper simply re-echoes it with "No more
secrets in the land!" (113) and "No more shall we allow one person to rule
our land for us!" (114).

One leaves Butake's plays with the feeling that hope in the liberation of the villages, the nation, has not been lost. It is only a matter of time and a change in tactics that true democracy, social justice, the rule of law, and all that goes with the pride of the human spirit or dignity will be regained. As in all his plays, Butake speaks the language of wisdom. No true freedom has ever been given on a platter of gold—it has always been fought for and bought with blood. This reminds us of the six innocent Cameroonians that were shot to death by government forces in Bamenda on May 26, 1990 when the opposition party, Social Democratic Front, was launched, and the others who have been killed or maimed in the struggle for authentic democracy recently in Ndu and other parts of Cameroon. Perhaps, it is time the Shey Ngongs gave way to the Mboysis and the Kwengongs to lead the fight for freedom and democracy. If the Kwifons and the Kibarankos have been neutralized, it is time the Fibuen took over.

Like Ngugi in *A Grain of Wheat* and *Petals of Blood*, Butake brilliantly brings to life a village community and places the lives of the villagers on the stage of national history. The villagers are inevitably swept into the revolutions that lead to the overthrow of dictatorship. The villagers of Ewawa, led by Kengong, declare the end of autocracy and a return to democracy. However, Butake does not advocate a return to the past; instead, he addresses the present and future of Ewawa, or rather Cameroon. So his plays are a direct challenge to the existing sociopolitical relationships that have combined to destitute the villagers of their God-given rights of liberty, freedom, justice, and the pursuit of happiness. The center of moral struggle in the plays is found in the struggle of the villagers, especially the women, to defend their land and fend off the intrusion of a rapacious and corrupt system led by the Fon, the Bororos, the police officers, the magistrates, and other authorities who undermine their source of subsistence and livelihood. In this struggle, the men become powerless and surrender their leadership position to women. Mboysi becomes the Cameroonian counterpart of the Kenyan Wanja—strong, self-assertive, resilient—who brings life back to the people. They both break relationships with forces of oppression and strike a blow against the oppressor. Butake's characterization of Mboysi as a force of change to reckon with corresponds to what Fanon identifies as the forbearer of the pre-revolutionary stage in which the task of the revolutionary writer is to envision for the people "all revolts, all desperate actions, all those abortive attempts drowned in rivers of blood" which eventually lead "to more widespread, organized, and effective forms of revolt."[13]

Butake is not only a social realist but a socialist realist, one who engages in writing literature of combat. He uses his plays to rip the veil of normalcy, respectability, and justice from the existing political order in his society (Cameroon) and to proclaim the duty of revolution. In fact, Ngugi's *Devil On the Cross*, in addressing the dilemma of the Kenyan people, indirectly addresses that of the Cameroonians, since both artists (Butake and Ngugi) share a common view of history:

> Our lives are a battle field on which is fought a continuous war between the forces that are pledged to confirm our humanity and those determined to dismantle it. . .those whose aim is to open our eyes, to make us see the light and look to tomorrow, asking ourselves about the future of our children, and those who wish to lull us into closing our eyes, encouraging us to care only for our stomachs today, without thinking about the tomorrow of our country. [14]

In fact, the battle is between the builders and sustainers of culture, on the one hand, and the oppressors and dismantlers of that culture, on the other, and Butake aligns himself with the people—those who do not only build the culture but equally fight to protect it and sustain it. Hence, the Cameroonian audience cannot help but see themselves in the mirror of Butake's plays. These fiery plays call for moral responsibility, for the natives to take up the challenge of national duty and eschew the politics of palm-wine, corruption, nepotism, and exploitation. Butake's plays therefore represent the transition from a literature that proclaims revolutionary truths to the production of a literature of action, one in which the action of creation is part of the process of organization for revolution. It is a call for literature of politics and literature as politics.

NOTES

1. Lapiro de Mbanga was a popular musician who was noted for his highly critical brand of music against the government of Cameroon. Unfortunately, prior to his death in 2014, he lost favor with the general public because of the belief that he had been bought over by the ruling CPDM party in Cameroon. His name was synonymous with bribery.

2. Joyce, James, *A Portrait of an Artist as a Young Man* (Cambridge: Cambridge University Press, 2004) 268.

3. Butake, Bole, *And Palm Wine Will Flow* in *Lake God and Other Plays* (Yaoundé: Editions CLE, 1999), 98–114. Further references to Butake's plays shall be taken from this edition and shall be cited in parenthesis henceforth in this chapter.

4. John Osborne, *Look Back in Anger* (London: Macmillan, 1956).

5. Neil Lazarus, "(Re)turn to the People: Ngugi wa Thiong'o and the Crisis of Postcolonial African Intellectualism." *The World of Ngugi wa Thiong'o*. Ed. Charles Cantalupo (Trenton, NJ: African World Press, 1995), 11–16.

6. George A. Panichas, *Prefatory Note: The Politics of Twentieth-Century Novelist* (New York: T.Y. Crowell, 1974), xviii.

7. Mark Schorer, *Sinclair Lewis: An American Life* (New York: McGraw-Hill Book Company, 1961), 356.

8. Ignazio Silone quoted in *The Politics of Twentieth-Century Novelists*, 81.

9. Joseph Takougang and Milton Krieger, *The African State and Society in the 1990s: Cameroon's Political Crossroads* (Boulder, CO: Westview Press, 1998).

10. William Shakespeare, *Macbeth*. Ed. Robert S. Miola (New York: W.W. Norton & Company, 2004), 5.3.23–31.

11. *Transparency International* http://www.transparencyinternational.org 1998 and 1999.

12. Paul Biya, *Communal Liberalism* (London : Macmillan, 1987). 114.
13. Frantz Fanon, *The Wretched of the Earth* (New York: Grove Press, 163). 207.
14. Ngugi wa Thiong'o, *Devil On the Cross* (London: Heinemann, 1982). 53.

FOUR

Re-Configuration of Colonialism in Postcolonial Cameroon in *Lake God and Other Plays*

The legacy European colonialism left on African countries is not only incontestable but lasting. Such legacy is manifested in the so-called civilized ways of constructing European style of houses, formal educational systems, the imposition of foreign languages on the business and administrative spheres of life, and a lifestyle at variance with the indigenous African lifestyles. While some African scholars and philosophers have welcomed these elements as beneficial to Africans, others have eschewed them as destructive of the African way. There has, therefore, arisen a continuous tension between the two groups whereby those who favor the foreign ways point to the advantages that accrue from colonialism, and, on the other hand, those who despise this unfortunate historical era point to the exploitative nature of the new ways. The latter group maintains that true colonialism had almost nothing positive to offer Africans.

According to Vincent Khapoya, the main objective of colonialism was the destruction of the colonized because "Colonial administrators often pursued policies that totally disregarded African interests and opinions—policies that removed colonized Africans as active participants in shaping their own history" (110).[1] Joseph Harris confirms Khapoya's theory by asserting that:

> The establishment of European colonial rule in Africa placed ultimate power in the hands of aliens who came from a cultural background that traditionally had denigrated African people. Thus the dominant long-range force became the colonial state that emphasized modern forms of . . . bureaucratic rule. Indigenous political and economic structures lost their legitimacy and authority. (206)[2]

It is, therefore, obvious that colonialism imposed the will of the colonizing Europeans on the formerly independent African people, with the explicit or sometimes implicit intention of exploiting the Africans economically, culturally, and politically. To succeed in doing so, the imperialists found it necessary to defend colonialism by promising the colonized "a higher order of existence" and by reassuring the domestic critics that, on the balance, the gains of the colonized far outweighed their losses; and by contending that at any rate the colonized were being saved from the brutality of their old life. The colonizers argued further that the colonized were being offered the blessings of a morally and technologically superior civilization. This concept was a very potent psychological propaganda which had a way of working on the minds of the colonized, destroying the confidence the colonized had in their way of life, institutions, and their creative abilities within their own cultures. The educated or rather literate elite therefore saw colonialism as conferring on them a higher social order, a higher and more advanced civilization, and a means of upgrading and maintaining their newly acquired status at the expense of their indigenous cultural values.

The colonized started off by acquiescing to the new dispensation through servitude with the aim of eventually inheriting the ways of the colonial authorities. Hence, the struggle for independence in the 1960s seemed to have been carried out with two objectives: on the one hand, there were those who sacrificed their lives to acquire genuine freedom from the colonial masters to truly liberate their lands from the domination of these foreigners, and, on the other hand, there were those opportunists who saw in this struggle an attempt simply to supplant the colonial masters in order to attain the status of their former masters with all the collateral benefits that accrue from such positions. This contradiction shocked Ernest A. Champion who had thought that "colonialism . . . was never meant to be a perpetual institution; it was not a timeless adventure" (77).[3] Unfortunately, he continues, "colonialism not only appropriated land from other nations, but there was also an attendant colonization of the mind, so much so that even after the demise of colonialism, the colonization of the mind continues" (73). It is indeed this "colonization of the mind" that negated and undercut the original concept of the fight for freedom, a fight which was meant to free the Africans from colonial rule and colonial mentality.

At independence, the hope of many African nation states was that they would extricate themselves from the inferiority mentality by replacing the colonial authorities with their own educated sons and daughters, many of whom had been educated and trained in Europe and the Americas. So independence was to spell the total death of colonialism and the colonial mentality. Unfortunately, this was not to be the case in most colonized nation states. This situation was particularly pervasive in Francophone Africa where the French colonial policy of assimilation attempted to create French people out of Africans. As President Paul Biya of Cameroon was to assert some years ago after having a working session with the former French president François Mitterrand, the independent leaders of French Africa remained students and stewards of their colonial masters. After meeting with the former French president François Mitterrand in Paris in 1991 to discuss the implementation and pursuit of democracy in Francophone African countries, Paul Biya said, over Cameroon Radio Television transmitted from Paris, that he is one of Mitterrand's best pupils (Takougang and Krieger 109).[4]

Though Biya might not have meant it in a literal sense, such a statement validates the colonial masters' stereotypical approach to Africa as a lost continent, where the natives are incapable of ruling themselves or understanding the concept of democracy. It is this same mentality that the prolific essayist and critic philosopher Frantz Fanon observed in Algeria in 1962 in the unfortunate turn of events following Algerian independence:

> [After the French were forced to leave], the elite layer of Europeans in Algeria was promptly supplanted by an elite layer of bourgeois Algerians who sought little more than to snatch appropriated privileges into their own hands. In this sense, colonialism went undefeated. Widespread poverty and social inequity persisted, and the manipulation of power ensured that the FLN remained an unchallenged political party in democratic Algeria in the following decades. Throughout the rest of Africa, similar tales played out: internal conflicts arose, mostly from economic and political strangleholds exacted upon these small nations by their former or continuing colonizers. (Ehlen 167)[5]

Fanon's experience was equally shared by the African-American dramatist LeRoi Jones whose inspiration for and "commitments to cultural nationalism" based on Africa's supposed "successful rebellions against colonial rule" were frustrated when he visited Africa in October 1974. He abandoned his stance when he saw that "a simple change in the complexion of power would not bring about the transformation for which he looked" (Bigsby 285).[6] Native Africans resorted to behaving like the White colonizers.

Furthermore, Khapoya, in his analysis of political instability in Africa, concluded that "the transfer of power by European colonialists did not lead to changes in the political institutions that the Africans inherited or in the basic orientation of ordinary people toward their new leaders wielding authority and power over them, whose primary objective was to serve vested interest rather than the country as a whole" (190–91).[7] A new breed of African leaders corrupted by power and fueled by greed took over from their colonial masters and continued the dehumanization of their fellow Africans, especially those who opposed or questioned their leadership style. It is, therefore, Frantz Fanon's reference to the new class of Algerians as "continuing colonizers" and LeRoi Jones' disappointment with postcolonial political configuration that have drawn acute attention to the re-figuration of colonialism as a negation of the self after the colonial masters left.

As Fanon eloquently alluded to in the passage above, the African nations were now to confront another colonial monster, the "able students" of the Masters who had so learned the tricks of the oppressors and combined with the native knowledge of their people that they set up and fortified themselves against their own people, exploiting and enslaving the people for their own personal gains. This political machination undercut the whole concept of political and economic freedom and independence. In the end, these leaders find themselves isolated by the local leaders and citizens, but surrounded by their political stooges who clamor for the proverbial "crumbs" that fall from the masters' tables. This, in a way, was not only a re-figuration of colonialism or what has become known as neo-colonialism, but equally a negation of the self, a self-denial of sorts. In other words, the new leaders betrayed the political, economic, and cultural platforms on which they had campaigned against the colonial masters. They now became the Black Masters (as opposed to the White Masters) and experts in the game of re-colonialism and the exploitation of the natives. This situation is vividly captured by Shey Ngong in Bole Butake's *And Palm Wine Will Flow* as he bewails the state to which the village has degenerated under the new political setup:

> What a land! What a people! To think that people in other lands . . .
> Oh! Nyombom!
> Creator and guardian of the land,
> Grant me strength and wisdom
> To weather the surging storm.
> The Fon has lost vision.
> The noble men and elders of this land
> Now listen only to the inner voice
> Of greed, and fear of a man who has
> Surrounded himself with listeners
> And watchdogs to do his bidding. (89)[8]

Later, Shey Ngong characterizes the land where the transvaluation of values has become the norm: "Today, nobles have become slaves and slaves nobles" (92), and the land has become one of "drinking and feasting where there is too much in the belly . . . [and the] head becomes an empty shell." Shey Ngong's use of the imagery of drinking and eating here is indeed a metaphor for the exploitation of the people by their own leaders, a theme adumbrated in Ayi Kwei Armah's *The Beautyful Ones Are Not Yet Born* (1968).[9]

The protest literature of postcolonial Cameroon and, by extension, Africa is replete with attempts of writers to reevaluate the fallouts of independence and to identify and apportion blame for the failure of dreams of freedom, liberty, equality, and the pursuit of happiness for all and sundry that had been promised at independence. The political leaders have become so comfortable with their present positions that they have resorted to exploiting the local people through fear, intimidation, coercion, bribery, and corruption and the outright rigging of national elections to ensure their continuity in power. To enhance continuous security and consolidation of power, the political leaders have resorted to tribalism, nepotism in the forms of regional, class, ethnic, socioeconomic status, language, and sometimes religious marginalization.

These colonial tendencies sometimes take the form of one group (region, ethnicity, class) imposing its will on the rest and thereby betraying the fundamental trust and confidence that had constituted the foundation on which the national unity was built. The other citizens who do not share the same ideology with the ruling class are automatically referred to as foreigners or strangers, as was the case between the ruling Beti ethnic group, on the one hand, and the Anglophone and Bamilike groups, on the other, in Cameroon in the early 1990s (Takougang and Krieger 95–97).[10] In response to the launching of the Social Democratic Front (SDF) in Bamenda in 1990, the late Mayor of Yaoundé, Emah Basile, blamed the uprisings and political protests that resulted from this political event on the Anglophones whom he called "les énemies dans la maîson" "les étrangers, les Nigériens," (translated as "the enemies in the house," "the strangers, the Nigerians" (94–96).[11]

The English-speaking Cameroonians, or the British Southern Cameroonians, could no longer accept the second-class status that was assigned to them and the resultant marginalization they suffered. In such cases, and when the people are politically sensitive (like in the Southern Cameroonian situation against La République du Cameroun), this has given rise to secessionist tendencies manifested in public demonstrations. In Cameroon, it culminated in the All Anglophone Conference I and II which took place in Buea and Bamenda in 1993 and 1994, respectively (Aka 291, Takougang and Krieger 168–69). See also Emmanuel A. Aka, *The British Southern Cameroons 1922–1961: A Study in Colonialism and Underdevelopment* (Plattville, WI: Nkamnje Global Tech, 2002).[12] Indeed, this acrimonious atmosphere provided the fertile grounds for Butake's politically charged play *Shoes and Four Men in Arms*.

Shoes and Four Men in Arms depicts a military dictatorship where the soldiers are sent to quell a popular uprising with unprecedented brutality. This event is reminiscent of the political uprisings and protests of the early 1990s sparked by the launching of the SDF and the call for a Sovereign National Conference.[13] In this play, the citizens come out shouting: "We want freedom! We want jobs! We want our salaries! Give us freedom! Liberty now! Freedom! Liberty! Freedom!" (141). In the late 1950s and early 1960s, one would have conceived this attitude in the context of the colonized rising against their foreign imperial overlords, but it is ironic that in this play, the natives are rising against their own national leaders. In fact, the citizens are clamoring for freedom and liberty from their own leaders who have literally reduced them to second-class citizens, slaves, and colonists. This cry for salaries is reminiscent of the experience of the teaching corps of the then University of Yaoundé who went for seven months without a salary. The general public service experienced a similar situation for a few months until the treasury found money to redress this very volatile situation. This political strife and unrest are the citizens' reactions to the exploitation they now suffer at the hands of their new "colonial" masters, their supposed leaders whom Butake now refers to, in *Dance of the Vampires,* as the vampires.

In a conversation between Nformi and Albinia (a nickname for Caucasians), Nformi uses this vampire imagery to draw an analogy between the exploitation of the natives both by the colonial masters and their protégés who have now constituted the ruling junta: "Albinia and their emissary, Albino, are only interested in *sucking* the wealth of our land, while Psaul Roi and Song are sucking the blood of the people" (172). Like with Fon Joseph, the president's name here is also very symbolic: the New Testament Saul was the persecutor of the early Christians in the biblical book of the Acts of the Apostles. Unfortunately, Albinia has not been able to convert him to the servant of the people like the biblical Saul was converted and later changed to Paul. Another dichotomy here is that while the New Testament Saul was a scholar, a philosophy, very intelligent, our Psaul Roi has no intellectual inclinations or ventures that will even convince his citizens, subjects, or the expatriate partners to honor him with the thought of a philosopher. Again, these western names are another domain where the African has enslaved himself or herself to colonialism by buying into a nomenclature which is both ridiculous, ironic, and contradictory to their real and true identities.

This vampire image ("sucking" imagery) is symbolic of the relationship that existed between the colonized and the colonizers wherein the colony existed to serve the material well-being of the colonizer. However, a much more devastating relationship now exists between the ruling elite and the natives where, in the absence of "the wealth of the land" (which has already been sucked by the Albinia, the white colonizers), Psaul Roi, the ruler, now sucks the blood of the people. Instead of giving life to the people, as has been the traditional role of the King, the King sucks life out of the people. Without blood, life ceases to exist. This, in effect, is the negation of the self, as this action is tantamount to self-destruction. In African cultures, the King usually stands for the people, and that is why he is usually addressed and referred to in the collective third person plural pronoun "they" or first person pronoun plural "we" or "us" even when he is alone. In fact, Albino refers to this self-destructive tendency of the king when he compares his foreign home palace (or seat of government) with that of Psaul Roi's:

> My assignment as an emissary to your kingdom was to explore the possibility of doing business with your people. After my brief stay here, there is no doubt that business opportunities abound. Even the insignificant but humanitarian affair of the incinerators has yielded and is still yielding a lot of dividends. Just as a ruler without the ruled is no ruler, so is the land without people, no matter how rich it may be. Your Most Royal Majesty, you turned against your people and now they won't come back in spite of your instruments and proclamations urging them to do so. Where I come from the palace is a market place where people converge to dialogue with their king. But here, the palace, like the land, has become the evil forest where people fear to tread. (171)

Albino's observation is an accurate depiction of the presidential palace in Yaoundé which is protected by mounted armed presidential guards, whose fearful presence has turned the palace into a proverbial "evil forest." It also adumbrates the theme of alienation which eventually resulted in separatist movements like the Southern Cameroons National Council (the SCNC), now known as the British Southern Cameroons Nation (BSCNATION), clamoring for independence from La République du Cameroun on the bases of regional and linguistic marginalization and incompatibility.

It is the same image and impression we have of the palace in *And Palm Wine Will Flow* where people go, not for advice and wisdom, but where, according to Shey Ngong, people "come to [the Fon] with gifts in return for the red feather" (91). The Fon is equally referred to as "Holy One, the Lion of Ewawa" who has pronounced that "the farmlands of [Shey Ngong's] revered wives now belong to Kibanya's wives" (93). There is also the prevalence of what the soldiers in *Shoes and Four Men in Arms* refer to as "Social malaise, agitations, and demonstrations" (140) resulting from the failure of the government to pay salaries, the rising unemployment, poverty, and military brutality meted against the unarmed civilians. University female students are mercilessly raped by the half-educated soldiers who force the students and university graduates to denigrate university education and literacy. They tell the unemployed graduates:

> Where are you, vandals? Subversive over-sabi bookshops! Come out and I will show you something. Standard Seven is better than big, big certificate. Big certificate, no work to do. So you become subversives and vandals and terrorists. (119).

The situation/incident captured above, which incidentally happened at the University of Yaoundé between 1990 and 1992 after the launching of the Social Democratic Front, approximates, though on a minor scale,

the complaint raised by the American colonies against the British colonizers in 1776: the turning of the local soldiers against their people making
the soldiers to become the executioners of their friends and brethren.
Butake may not have had this analogy in mind by the time of writing, but
it will be deceptive not to see this parallel. The gravity of the whole
situation in the play does not only lie in the barbaric treatment the natives
are subjected to, but in the fact that, unlike in the American colonies
where the ruler was foreign, in this play, the King here is one of them.
The King has turned against his own people. The number of shoes gath-
ered by the soldiers signifies the number of students who have been
savagely disposed of as revealed in this gory conversation among the
merciless soldiers:

> First: How many did we capture during the operation?
> Third: Who cares to count? Four or five truck loads. Something like
> that.
> First: Any girls?
> Second: Plenty. You know they are more easily affected by tear gas.
> And since we surrounded them completely it was by far better to catch
> a girl. (118)

The soldiers then proceed to loot shoes, appliances, and extort money
from the helpless civilians under the guise of quelling an uprising. In this
dramatic narrative above, we see Butake interfacing art with reality and
marrying reality with art, where the literary artist and historian are one,
united in a frontal attack on an inhumane political setup.

It is indeed a misreading of the play to conclude that "these soldiers
serve their country by standing guard over a pile of shoes, the only visible trace of the demonstration" (Breitinger 14).[14] This myopic approach
begs the question: whose interest are the soldiers serving and what do the
shoes represent? The soldiers serve a double interest here. In the first
place, the soldiers are there, as Albino says, to execute the orders of the
General (President) whose survival is threatened:

> [The Chief Commander] means privileges and honours which regular
> soldiers like you don't have and will never dream of having. Yet he and
> the monarch are completely dependent on the army, on you, to do their
> dirty job of keeping the people under an iron heel. We are talking about
> the plight of your people. The manipulation of you soldiers by one
> man, an alcoholic who happens also to be drunk with power even if he
> doesn't know what to do with it. (167)

Secondly, the soldiers use this opportunity to rape girls and loot property
from houses they have broken into for their insatiable sexual and material greed. These soldiers are indeed a refined rendition of the police officer
in *The Survival* who uses his position of power to rape and extort sexual
favors from Mboysi. Mboysi's reaction to and description of the situation
parallels the despicable and nauseating language Armah uses in *The*

Beautyful Ones Are Not Yet Born to describe the corrupt pot-bellied politicians. After having outwitted the police officer, Mboysi addresses him:

> You would kill me, would you? You crawling, thieving maggot. Growing rich on the misfortunes of others. Stuffing your decaying stomach and your bulging pockets on the calamity of my people. Never again shall you live to perpetuate our misery. It was better for all of us to have been killed than to be treated like caged animals. (83)

And where the officers cannot rape or extract sexual favors from the poor women, they openly ask for bribes to perform the duties for which they are paid; sometimes, they flagrantly break or operate above the law. This is the case with the "practical philosopher" in Butake's other play *The Rape of Michelle* where, without any moral compunction, the police officer asks for a bribe from Akwen who wants to visit her incarcerated husband:

> Policeman: Madam, I will not do you a favour for nothing. You think I am alone on duty? There are three others out there. What you are giving me cannot buy a bottle of red wine.
> Akwen: Alright, here is something for all of you. And, please, treat my husband well.
> Policeman: It all depends on you, Madam. Our treatment of your husband depends on you. . . . Don't stay too long. Or you will put me into trouble. The law says that criminals must never be left alone with visitors. (180)

Later, the policeman reports to Mikindong (Akwen's husband) that he had told the latter's wife that everything depended on her, "And she did her duty. And now you are happy. That is how life should be. You make me happy. I make you happy. One hand washes the other. And that is how things should be" (183). This is a case of extreme perversion of justice. The case of the one hand washing another is a philosophical assertion of the reciprocity of life instilled into the mind to understand that every good deed is rewarded positively. It also suggests the notion of collaboration and cooperation to encourage the cultivation of good and praiseworthy deeds and behavior, but in this case polluted to encode corruption. This seems to be a pervasion of language and philosophy which has been created and twisted into some form of euphemism for bribery and corruption. This usage obtains its meaning from a context best understood by the citizens. Indeed, this linguistic ingenuity is masterfully displayed by Policeman who schools Mikindong on practical philosophy:

> Teacher, let me tell you something. Whether you did it or not does not really matter. If you do not make contacts, you are going to stay in prison for a good part of your only life. . . . But with money . . . you can move mountains . . . Contacts. That is the right word. . . . A telephone call from above to the magistrate! An envelope from below to the mag-

istrate! And the deed is done. The case is closed or simply thrown out of court. Contacts. . . . Oh yes! We must be practical and realistic. You think the magistrate eats truth? You think the prosecutor eats truth? You think the commissioner eats truth? But people need a drink now and again. They need money to do things. That is what I call practical philosophy. (186)

The soldiers, the police officers, and the court system who constitute part of the legacy bequeathed by the white colonial masters are used here not to preserve order or guarantee and uphold justice like the colonial masters had conceived (Sandbrook 147),[14] but rather to intimidate and punish the political agitators and supposed criminals who are fighting for their legitimate rights and freedoms. They are a reflection of a system of governance that is self-destructive, one that negates the very concept of a government of the people, for the people, by the people.

Indeed, A. Adu Boahen discusses the irony of independence when he maintains that the greatest loss for Africa resulting from colonialism was "the loss of sovereignty and independence by the colonized peoples. This loss of sovereignty in turn, implied the loss of the right of a state to control its own destiny; to plan its own development; to decide which outside nations to borrow from or to associate with or emulate . . ." (99).[15] Again in *Dance of the Vampires*, Albino reiterates the King's responsibility: "Your Excellency the Most Royal, there is no business without trust, without goals. Your goal is your throne, power. Mine is gain. Shall we seal with a handshake?" (166). Albino understands the desire of Psaul Roi's mind, which is to wield and exercise absolute power over his impoverished subjects, rather than to protect them. Later, Albino underscores the nonchalant attitude of the King and his supporters in these words:

> What wonderful predators you are! Preying on your own kind. Don't you see the consequences of your own folly? I have had to bring in specialists from Albinia to build the incinerator and to fell the trees for wood and transport it to the various locations. And here you are asking me for more compensations. You ask your Chief Commander here, or your Commander in Chief who has barricaded himself in his palace and is drinking himself to certain death, what the real situation of your beloved country is. (166)

We are confronted here again with the image of eating (if not cannibalism: "predators," "preying on your own kind") and "drinking"—a callous disregard for the well-being of the citizens, a scene of plenty in the midst of poverty. The answer to Albino's worry about the true state of the beloved country is obvious: abject poverty, social unrest and rebellion. This is a country with a government where the soldiers are manipulated by "one man, an alcoholic who happens to be drunk with power even if he doesn't know what to do with it."

As a consequence, many intellectuals have gone on self-exile, proclaiming that "until the monarch leaves they will remain refugees. They have never been ruled by a vampire king" (167). This indeed is the land of the big dogs where the concepts of freedom, equality, and the pursuit of happiness have been negated and reduced to self-destruction, a self-negation of sorts.

NOTES

1. Vincent B. Khapoya, *The African Experience: An Introduction*. Second Edition. (Upper Saddle River, NJ: Prentice Hall, 1998).

2. Joseph E Harris, *Africans and Their History*. 2nd Edition. (New York: Meridian, 1998).

3. Ernest A. Champion, *Mr. Baldwin, I Presume: James Baldwin–Chinua Achebe: A Meeting of the Minds* (New York: University Press of America, Inc. 1995). The conversation between Achebe and Baldwin brought out many points of convergence of ideas, especially the concept of the "Otherness" of people though they sometimes disagreed on the concept of the way forward for African development.

4. Joseph Takougang and Milton Krieger, *African State and Society in the 1990s: Cameroon's Political Crossroads* (Boulder, CO: Westview Press, 1998), 109.

5. Patrick Ehlen, *Frantz Fanon: A Spiritual Biography* (New York: The Crossroad Publishing Company, 2000).

6. Christopher W. E. Bigsby, *Modern American Drama: 1945–2000* (Cambridge: Cambridge University Press, 2000).

7. Khapoya, 190–91.

8. Bole Butake, *Lake God and Other Plays* (Yaounde, Cameroon: Editions CLE, 1999). This is a collection of all of Bole Butake's major plays. All further citations from Butake's plays shall be taken from this edition.

9. Ayi Kwei Armah, *The Beautyful Ones Are Not Yet Born* (London: Heinemann, 1968).

10. Takougang and Krieger, 95–97.

11. Peter Geschiere has elaborated extensively on this theme of exclusion in his discussion of the dichotomy between belonging and not belonging, the natives versus the "foreigners," which became a passionate cry to dispossess the wealthy Bamilikes and Anglophones who lived and constructed personal and business houses in Yaoundé, the political capital of Cameroon. The latter ethnicities and language groups were accused of spearheading the political uprisings orchestrated by the launching of the SDF party in Bamenda. All Bamilkes and especially English-speaking Cameroonians were persecuted as "strangers," Nigerians, and the "enemies in the house." See more in Geschiere's *The Perils of Belonging: Autochthony Citizenship, and Exclusion in Africa & Europe* (Chicago: University of Chicago Press, 2009). Neil Lazarus sees Ngugi engaged in a similar situation and resistance in "(Re)turn to the People: Ngugi wa Thiong'o and the Crisis of Postcolonial African Intellectualism." *The World of Ngugi wa Thiong'o*. Ed. Charles Cantalupo (Trenton, NJ: African World Press, 1995), 11–26.

12. Takougang and Krieger, 168–69.

13. Eckhard Breitinger, "Bole Butake's Strategies as a Political Playwright." *The African Theatre: Playwrights and Politics*. Eds. Martin Banham, James Gibbs, and Femi Osofsan (Oxford: James Currey Ltd., 2001), 7–17.

14. Richard Sandbrook, *The Politics of Africa's Economic Stagnation* (New York: Cambridge University Press, 1985), 147.

15. A. Adu Boahen, *African Perspective on Colonialism* (Baltimore: John Hopkins University Press, 1987), 98–100. Also see Frantz Fanon's *The Wretched of the Earth*. (New York: Grove Press, Inc. 1968).

FIVE

Colonial Legacy and the Culture of Corruption in *Lake God* and *The Rape of Michelle*

Colonialism radically and chaotically transformed Africa politically because the political set up left behind by the receding colonial authorities was radically different from that which the colonizers met on arrival in Africa. Essentially, two types of political systems existed in precolonial Africa: the States and the Stateless Societies. According to Vincent Khapoya," States were organized structurally in much the same way as modem states. Bureaucracies carried out certain functions such as collecting taxes, supervising ceremonies, entertaining signatories, and compelling people to do what the kings or chiefs wanted them to do." On the other hand, the "stateless" societies were politically decentralized entities, had no bureaucracies . . . and tended to be based on kinship (i.e., lineage systems and extended families) (61).[1] But these organizations were based on and obtained their legitimacy from two key concepts: values and authority patterns. They were highly respected and the people often prostrated before them to show their respect and reverence. The king and his council of elders were sovereign and were entrusted with the sacred responsibility of maintaining law and order, settling disputes among lineages, especially over land and property. The prosperity of their land was their primary concern and responsibility. In other words, they existed to look after the interest and the welfare of their citizens.

However, these political arrangements were to change with the coming of colonialism. European colonialism came therefore to undermine the legacies of nineteenth-century African development by denying Africans and their traditional rulers sovereignty over their own lands by "establishing entirely new principles of colonial authority and by restruc-

turing Africa's internal political set-ups" (Khapoya 110). Khapoya further
maintains that because of this racialist attitude, "colonial administrators
often pursued policies that totally disregarded African interests and
opinions—policies that removed colonized Africans as active participants
in shaping their own history." Joseph Harris confirms this assertion when
he declares that

> The establishment of European colonial rule in Africa placed ultimate
> power in the hands of aliens who came from a cultural background
> that traditionally had denigrated African people. Thus the dominant
> long-range force became the colonial state that emphasized modern
> forms of . . . bureaucratic rule. Indigenous political and economic struc-
> tures lost their legitimacy and authority. (206)[2]

This inferiority/superiority complex and reconfiguration of this
master/servant relation became the dominant determinant of the relationship between the colonized and the colonizer (and, by extension, the
white masters and the black servants). Furthermore, the colonial arrangement thrived on the economic exploitation of African states buttressed by
living standards that were not in consonance with the traditional standards of living. It created another class system which grouped the societies into the haves and the have-nots, where the have-nots are subjected
to beggarly existence and misery. According to Jean-Paul Sartre, "colonialism denies human rights to human beings whom it has subdued by
violence, and keeps them by force in a state of misery and ignorance that
Marx would rightly call a subhuman condition." (xxiv).[3] This situation is
further adumbrated by Franz Fanon in his two works *Black Skin, White
Masks* (1952) and *The Wretched of the Earth* (1963),[4] wherein he discusses
the devastating and inhuman relation between the colonizers and the
colonized where the latter group is constantly subjected to inferior and
mentally dehumanizing situations. The colonized, therefore, are forced
into looking up to their colonial masters as liberators, demigods upon
whom they have to depend for protection and sustenance.

To succeed in this potent dehumanization of the colonized, the impe-
rialist found it necessary to defend colonialism "to internal critics of the
system and the colonized by promising the latter a higher order of existence; by trying to convince them and to re-assure domestic critics that,
on the balance, the gains of the colonized will far outweigh their losses;
and by contending that at any rate they are being saved from the brutality of their old life and offered the blessings of a morally and technologically superior civilization" (Obiechina 68).[5] This was a very effective
psychological propaganda that had a way of working on the minds of the
colonized, destroying the confidence the colonized had in their original
way of life, institutions, and their creative abilities within their own cultures. The colonized, especially the elite, therefore saw colonialism as
conferring a higher order of social organization, a higher civilization, and

a means of refining and upgrading their cultural life at the expense of their traditional or indigenous cultural values and political set-ups.

Being educated, in the European sense, propelled the elite to advantageous positions compared with the rest of the uneducated people. This elite class was equally aware of their African culture and the need to balance this against their newly acquired identity. They were therefore trapped in a many-sided dilemma in which they wished to identify with the traditional life and culture, while at the same time being repelled by a new system they hardly fully understood but enjoyed from their identification with the system. They recognized the ambivalence of their relationship with Western Civilization, but, at the same time, their deepest instinct of self-preservation told them that, although their hold on this civilization was vestigial, it represented their only substantial anchor. To renounce Western life and culture for a purely traditional way of life was tantamount to giving up something they already possessed for something that was hypothetically theirs. It amounted to sacrificing an intellectually satisfying position for what Obiechina calls "a persistent but largely emotional pressure" (69).[6] At the same time, in their attempt to hold on to illusory power which was gradually ebbing away, they resorted to a culture of bribery and corruption and the creation of cultic societies where members pledged to defend the "cause."

It is against the backdrop of the above transformation on both the rural and urban administrations that Bole Butake's *Lake God* (rural) and *The Rape of Michelle*[7] are set. These plays depict the extent to which the leaders will go in an attempt to hold to power as a form of self-preservation and legitimacy: they expend their energies devising and perfecting their newfound culture of corruption while ignoring the suffering of the marginalized masses. In the rural plays, Butake calls for the overthrow of the corrupt dictators, but in the urban centers such an appeal is nonexistent because of the machinery of the powerful and sometimes willing accomplices of the corrupt judiciary, who are now using bribery as a form of lifestyle, an investment of sorts.

Lake God opens on a note of confrontation between the Fon and Father Leo, the missionary, on the one hand, and the chief priest of the lake, Shey Bo-Nyo who stands for tradition and local culture, on the other. The stage directions emphasize this dichotomy by depicting the local Fon adorned not in traditional regalia, but in Western costume: "Stage decoration should reflect the Fon's bias for Western civilization at the expense of traditional culture. Even his costume reflects his obsession with Western culture. He is receiving a missionary, Father Leo" (9). This chief's preference for or even obsession with Western civilization confirms Obiechina's contention that this attitude is borne of the legacy of colonization whereby the colonizers portrayed their culture as superior to the African culture thereby undercutting the cultural values that gave the Africans their identity, legitimacy and real power. It equally, though regrettably, validates Molefi Asante's assertion that "Western-oriented scholars [and by extension chiefs] believe that the African needs to exhibit Western traits of thought and culture in order to be considered advanced" (194–95).[8] By adopting a Western name and adorning his palace in Western regalia, Fon Joseph is, in fact, succumbing to what Edem Kodjo calls" the image of others:"

> By imitating the culture of the other at all levels, by making himself an image of the other at all costs, by making his personality a reflection of the foreign . . . the African, having adopted social terms of foreign origin . . . believes that he has found a poise and strength for his spirit in a mimicry that only goes to the making of . . . derelict societies. . . . Standing as they do today as the image of the other, and by unimaginatively copying the sociohistorical experiences of peoples outside, Africans themselves are working for the destruction of their identity, to depersonalize themselves . . . (121).[9]

There is, in fact, a close affinity between Fon Joseph's Western style image and that of President Paul Biya on a billboard, as described by Joseph Takougang and Milton Krieger, looking "other than presidential in formal European style" and displayed everywhere else dressed "in a dark suit and tie" (217).[10] Shey Bo-Nyo warns the Fon, who is very reluctant to receive him in the presence of Father Leo, that "The white man has brought trouble to the land. He has killed our gods and the Fon is impotent" (9). The Fon who should traditionally surround himself with the council of the wise has instead surrounded "himself with thugs and sons of whores and people who will kill us and destroy our land" (9). Father Leo's reaction to Shey's outburst is typical of the colonizer's attitude: "What trouble have I brought to this village? The church has brought new life and progress to this village. And yet he says the white man will kill people and destroy the land. Sheer madness" (10). In reaction to the beating meted to Shey by the Fon's thugs, Father Leo concurs that, "That seems to be the only language that will pacify him. In civilized society he would be chained in a home for the mentally disturbed" (10). Father Leo projects himself here as what Albert Memmi calls the purported "custodian of the values of civilization and history" who "has the immense merit of bringing light to the colonized's ignominious darkness" (75).[11] The Fon immediately swings over to Father Leo's defense by saying, "We will never catch up with Europe, Father. We will never catch up. Thank God you came. Praise be to Jesus who sent out his disciples to convert the heathen" (10).

The Fon's concept of "[catching] up with Europe," which unfortunately is one of the destructive elements of colonial legacy, is, in fact, one of the problems which Franz Fanon diagnosed as inimical to the progress of Africa. In *The Wretched of the Earth* (1958), Fanon asserted:

> When I search for Man in the technique and the style of Europe, I see only a succession of negations of man. . . . Let us decide not to imitate Europe; let us try to create the whole man, whom Europe has been incapable of bringing to triumphant birth (391).[12]

Hence, Fon Joseph's attempt to "imitate" Europe is existentially a negation and an undermining of his personality and the traditional institution of fondom which he represents and a legitimization of the so-called civilizing mission of colonialism (Bohannan and Curtin 8–9).[13] Fon Joseph thus succumbs to what Memmi calls "the most serious blow" caused by colonialism: "being removed from history and from the community" (91). Butake definitely chose the biblical name of Joseph ironically. The biblical Joseph was favored by his father and the Egyptians because of his uprightness and clairvoyance, his prophetic disposition (Genesis 37–50). Our Fon Joseph lacks the integrity and moral rectitude ascribed to his biblical namesake. He is really the antithesis of the biblical Joseph, for instead of saving his people, he sells them and their land and betrays the trust and confidence placed in him. He uses his political power here for his personal aggrandizement and protection against his own people.

Furthermore, Fon Joseph's inferiority complex is a direct heritage of the colonial mentality which, according to Memmi, is built on three major ideological components: "the gulf between the culture of the colonialist and the colonized; . . . the exploitation of these differences for the benefit of the colonialist; [and] . . . the use of these supposed differences as standards of absolute fact" (71).[14] And as if to wake up from his delusion, the Fon tells Father Leo that Shey will never be converted because he is the priest of the lake god just like Father Leo is the priest of the Almighty God in heaven. Immediately Father Leo detects an attitude of ambivalence in the Fon and he proceeds to scold, chastise and school the Fon in the following exchange:

> Father Leo: How dare you, Fon! How dare you make such a comparison! In spite of all my efforts? In spite of all that I have done for you? You even dare to make reference to idols in my presence?
>
> Fon: Sorry, Father. I am very sorry, Father. Very, very sorry, Father. It was a slip of the tongue.
>
> Father Leo: My dear Fon, you must choose between Satan and God. Why do you allow such evil thoughts to bother you? It must be Lucifer . . . (10)

They then kneel and pray "Our Father. May the Almighty Father look with compassion upon his servant, Fon Joseph, and give him the strength to stand up against Lucifer and his evil gang!" (10–11).

In the above prayer, it is obvious that the lake god is Lucifer and Shey and his followers are "Lucifer's evil gang." Here we see Fon Joseph trampling on the sacred tradition that put him in power and from which he draws traditional power and respect simply because he wants to please Father Leo, the colonial master. Secondly, he has taken up a Western name to identify with and to pay his new allegiance to the colonizers. Unfortunately, he does not know or live to the full meaning of that biblical name, the Covenant of God. In Fanon's "Letter to The Resident Minister (1956)"[15] announcing his resignation in Algeria, Fanon referred to the endemic sickness where natives have become "decerebralized" (389). The Fon has become "decerebralized" by alienating himself from his cultural and traditional roots, and even from his people to serve a foreign god, considered to be superior and almighty. To the Fon, the power and authority which had formerly been vested on him by the local people (now called "Lucifer and his gang") now come from Father Leo and the Almighty God. The Fon is promised assistance because of his "progressive rule and respect for the civilized world" (11).

The real trouble and true test of the Western power comes immediately Father Leo leaves the Fon alone to test his fidelity to his new political and religious dispensations. His first test comes in reaction to the song of the women's secret cult, the Fibuen. He cannot handle the effrontery of the women and he reacts angrily: "What could be the meaning of this? The Fibuen in the kingdom of an enlightened Christian monarch? That must be . . ." (14). However, he is told that the women are coming into the palace with a dead body, and that culturally "the Fon does not see a corpse and live." Fon Joseph succumbs to this warning and orders the doors to the palace barred. Here we see that his cards of Western civilization and new religion start collapsing, as he bends to the superstition that is at variance with Christianity. As the Fon regains his posture, he is confronted by the women who pay him the traditional homage with "their hands on their knees in reference to the throne . . . The women prostrate and ululate as the Fon enters." They have bound and brought Dewa, the cattle rearer to the Fon to chastise him for allowing his cattle destroy their crops. Instead of receiving this honor in reverence to the culture of the people, the Fon again puts on his Western defiance:

> How many times must I tell you that this is a Christian kingdom? How often must I drive it into your heads that the heathen era of idol worship is history? How many times must I decree that the age of savagery and jungle law is over and done with in this land? (14)

The women's problem with Dewa is not only that his cattle have destroyed their crops, but that he has equally trampled on local authority by calling the Fon by name and revealing that he wields a certain amount of power over the Fon. At this point, Butake introduces the twin theme of corruption and abuse of power as it soon becomes clear that the Fon's refusal to send Dewa away from the land is aligned with the corrupt deals both of them have entered into. Again, he abuses his authority by forcing Dewa to accept that Dewa's cattle, not his, destroyed the women's crops. He then tells Dewa in pidgin English to pay compensation to the women for the destroyed crops. The unfortunate thing here is that Fon Joseph takes advantage of the reverence the women have for him and the women's illiteracy to enrich himself. Thus, he tells Dewa:

> You go muf two cow fo you nyun puttam for me nyun. Woman cow wey get leke three year so dat small tam dem get belle. You don hear fine? (18)
> (Translated: You go and remove two cows from your own herd and put into mine. They should be mature female cows of three years old, which will soon be pregnant. Do you understand me well?)

Fon Joseph has not only deprived the women of the meager sum of money Dewa has been charged for allowing the cattle to damage their crops, but he has taken advantage of this unfortunate situation to enrich himself through bribery and corruption. The underlying implication here is that Fon Joseph has inherited a colonial lifestyle that will require a constant supply of money and bribery to maintain. By so doing, he has adulterated the sacred trust that was subsumed in the legacy of the traditional chieftaincy. However, in the course of his actions, he loses the respect of his subjects and of Dewa, too.

Fon Joseph succeeds in his effrontery because he still represents to the women the traditional head whose divine responsibility is to protect and safeguard the lands of his subjects. This is a sacred trust that was handed to him by his forefathers and confirmed, respected and consolidated by his subjects. The betrayal of this trust carries a heavy sentence, one of which is the loss of the traditional respect of his subjects. Moreover, as Fon Joseph descends to the level of his partner in bribery, Dewa sees and uses his vulnerability against him. That is why the women complain that when they first threatened him with reprisal from the Fon, he called the Fon by his name. The love of money and a luxurious Western lifestyle have connived to divest the Fon of the reverence of his people. He becomes not Joseph the "Covenant" and liberator of the people from starvation; rather, he is the Judas Iscariot who sells the crops and respect of his people for the meager money and cows that the cattle grazers bribe him with. Like in the biblical parable of the sower, the Fon reaps from where he did not sow, and natural justice will pursue him and precipitate his downfall.

In *The Rape of Michelle*, the scene shifts to the urban center, the city where the political set-up is different. We may want to call it the modern or European style city where the three branches of government (the executive, the judicial, and the legislative) have been set up supposedly to protect the citizens and guarantee their freedoms and rights. This urban set-up is purely a Western concept and there people look for ways to relieve the tension of office work in bars. One of the evils brought about by this so-called urbanization is unemployment and prostitution. After work, Mikindong and his friends go to a chicken parlor (an informal drinking/eating joint) where they meet Rufina and her daughter Michelle. Rufina has always had a crush on Mikindong, their neighbor and teacher whose moral rectitude has always prevented him from any erotic relationship with her. No sooner do the gentlemen settle down for a beer than Michelle starts flirting with Mikindong, who rebuffs such advances on the basis of Michelle's tender age. Michelle's coquettish antics and attitude towards Mikindong ignite a conflict between her and the mother:

> Rufina: Every time my customers come here you want to show them that you are young and more beautiful. But I am telling you that if I ever hear that you and teacher have done anything . . . that day you will go.
>
> Michelle: But it's you who say he likes me!
>
> Rufina: I don't care. But I am telling you now that I like him. If he doesn't like me and prefers you, we will see. (178)

Rufina's threats are not idle, because the entire play is played out against the backdrop of Rufina's Machiavellian attempt to carry her threats through. It is unfortunate and scandalous that this game of survival is between mother and daughter who have completely ignored the decency of sexuality where relatives of the same blood, let alone mother and daughter, cannot date or engage in any sexual transaction with the same male. This subversion or challenge of cultural values embodied in this game of survival is often blamed on colonialism which revealed cases of first cousins and stepdaughters being raped by or getting married to each other or stepfathers, respectively.

Suddenly, we find Mikindong incarcerated for trumped-up charges that he raped Michelle. These fake charges and the court system become the arena in which a much more sophisticated culture of bribery and corruption is manifested. Mikindong has been refused bail because "Michelle's mother is determined to see that [Mikindong] serves a good term in prison. She is always in the Commissioner's office" (179). The policeman's declaration presupposes that Rufina has "bought" the Commissioner to keep Mikindong in prison, violating his rights to fair trial. And this is corruption at its highest, in a country that does not subscribe to speedy trial and protection under any constitutional amendments or Bill of Human Rights.

In a corrupt system of justice, the agents of justice all become accomplices in the culture of corruption. This becomes very evident in the policeman's attitude toward Akwen, Mikindong's wife, who has come to visit her husband. The conversation between the police and Akwen reveals a situation where the agents of justice have the effrontery to bend the law without any moral compunctions. After Mikindong asks his wife to give the policeman "some money for beer" in order to make his stay in jail more comfortable, they engage in the tactics of bribery and corruption:

> Policeman: Madam, I will not do you a favor for nothing you think I am here alone? There are three others out there. You saw them with your own eyes. What you are giving me cannot even buy a bottle of red wine.

> Akwen: Alright, here is something for all of you. And, please, treat my husband well.

> Policeman: It all depends on you, madam. Our treatment of your husband depends on you. You can even bring him a blanket and a tiny mattress, if you wish. But I have told you, there are four of us on duty. Yes, everything depends on you.

> Akwen: Please, I will do anything to make him comfortable.

> Policeman: Now you begin to understand. Bring the things at night. When there are not many people again in the station. Your husband is not just anybody and he deserves good treatment. That is why he is in this cell alone. Go to other cells and you will see fifty people. They are packed like sardines. But, as I said, it all depends on you. Don't stay too long or you will put into trouble. The law says that criminals must never be left alone with visitors. (180)

This verbal exchange between the policeman and Akwen is eloquent testimony of the nuances of the culture of corruption. A cursory look at the situation would reveal that the policeman cares about the law, but the underlying meaning of the exchange reveals that the policeman has carefully put into play a ploy to extort money from the poor woman in exchange for being "good" to her husband. This scenario is repeated when Zende, the attorney for Mikindong, visits Mikindong in prison. He gives the policeman more money to go "buy a packet of cigarettes." The attorney does not only bribe the policeman before having access to his client, but he equally informs Mikindong that he had to bribe the Court Registrar "thirty thousand francs" to schedule the hearing for "the day after tomorrow"(184). However, the outcome of the case will be decided by how many people connected to the legal system and the courts, in particular, Mikindong's team sees; that is buying off people because nobody will believe Mikindong's story in court:

> Mikindong: You know yourself that the law is what it is. Many innocent people get convicted while criminals go scot-free. All I ask of you is to make contacts with the presiding magistrate. I know he will like an envelope. My wife has promised to see him.

> Zende: I agree with you. It is a question of seeing people. Luckily for you, the magistrate is a personal friend of mine. We are on very good terms. But the prosecutor, Traisel, is a beast. As far as he is concerned,

you are already a criminal and condemned. I wonder how much she gave him. (185).

As Zende prepares to leave Mikindong, the latter reminds him: "But remember your own role. Contacts." On overhearing the above, the policeman seizes on the word "contacts" to elaborate what he calls "practical philosophy":

Policeman: That is the right word. Contacts. A telephone from above to the magistrate! An envelope from below to the magistrate! And the deed is done. The case is closed or simply thrown out of Court. Contacts!

Zende: I see you are a very practical philosopher.

Policeman: Oh yes! We must be practical and realistic. You think the Magistrate eats truth? You think the prosecutor eats truth? You think the commissioner eats truth? Nobody eats truth. But people need a drink now and again. They need money to do things. That is what I call practical philosophy. . . . Teacher, let me tell you something. Whether you did it or not does not really matter. If you do not make contacts, you are going to stay in prison for a good part of your life. And what will happen to your beautiful wife and work? She will become the woman of some powerful man. But with money . . . you can move mountains. (185–86)

The above dialogue captures the whole concept of corruption and the travesty of justice in Cameroon. It also reveals the extent to which common inventions such as envelopes and telephones have been converted to facilitators of the culture of corruption. To an outsider, they represent gadgets of communications and privacy, but to the local folk they are the coded messages of corruption and the distortion of justice. In fact, they have become symbols of bribery and corruption.

In his message to the prime minister of Cameroon during the latter's visit to Bamenda, North West Province on April 11, 2001, the head of the Human Rights Defense Group, the late Albert Mukong had the following to say to the Prime Minister:

We talk often of Cameroon as a peaceful country. Do we really have peace or we are simply exploiting a peace loving people? We believe that we can only achieve peace through justice, but we are worried to note that in the overall administration of the national territory justice doesn't seem to be playing an important role. We often refer to Cameroon as a state in which the rule of law applies but our study reveals Cameroon as a State in which the arbitrary reigns and the Rule of Law has no place. . . . Justice is a commodity in Cameroon available to the highest bidder. . . . The North West is not free from this racketeering of justice. . . . The lack of professional etiquette on the part of our judiciary has resulted in hundreds of suspects or accused persons being held up in waiting trial section in the prisons for many years. Another factor

promoting this situation is the indifference of Police and Gendarme
Officers towards investigation. . . . In general, the police are also expecting cash from the suspects so as to enable them proceed with the inves-
tigations. (SCNCFORUM Re:[africadaily3] HRDG's letter to the Prime
Minister of Cameroon: 1–2, 4/11/01; 5:47 p.m.)[16]

Mukong was adamant in accusing the president of promoting a culture of
corruption and encouraging the rule of lawlessness, which was tantamount to the display of "the lack of professional etiquette" on the part of
the judiciary or the court systems. This picture makes Minkindong's case
much more serious and as an arena in which to try this travesty of justice.

Mikindong can only win the case, not because he was innocent (because the policeman warned: the magistrate, the prosecutor and the commissioner do not eat the truth), but simply on the grounds of "bidding"
higher than Rufina and Michelle in this game of corruption. In fact, Mikindong's incarceration validates Mukong's assertion that rights of suspects are blatantly ignored and that justice is being racketeered. Hence,
when the magistrate delays or holds back passing judgment on the day of
the hearing, it is simply a trick to give Minkindong the chance to come up
with a "bigger envelope." The Magistrate waves Mikindong's life in his
face as a way to raise the stakes of the bargain for Mikindong and his
group. The magistrate does not make a secret of this as he complains to
his partner-in-crime and Mikindong's attorney Zende, on seeing the lavish celebration of Mikindong's appointment that coincides with his being
released from jail while awaiting sentencing: "With all this celebration
and the champagne popping all over, you think they can still put together something reasonable?" (198). The "something reasonable" here refers
to the bribe he is expecting from Mikindong. The partners in bribery and
corruption have ingeniously come up with a coded language, thereby
building an entire culture around corruption. At Mikindong's celebration, the magistrate reminds him in very diplomatic terms what he has at
stake:

> Mr. Mikindong, again I want to congratulate you most heartily. In fact,
> I do so from the bottom of my heart. That [being appointed principal] is
> not a job that one should lose by going to jail. Mrs. Mikindong, thank
> you very much for your kindness. Good night. (199)

The magistrate literally threatens Mikindong with continuous imprisonment and the deprivation of his family and the new job if Mikindong
does not offer a reasonable bribe equivalent in value to those things he
stands to lose when he goes to prison.

The above excerpt reveals the extent to which the judiciary will stoop
to extract a bribe from the innocent people. According to Zende, Mikindong's real trial begins from this moment of his temporary release from
jail and the field of combat is the arena of bribery and corruption. So his
cry: "But why should a man suffer so much and lose so much money

even though he is innocent" (199) is a cry of the helpless who are at the
mercy of the powerful. However, he is equally an accomplice as he promises Zende, though grudgingly, "However, I will do everything possible.
How much do you think he will be willing to accept?" He is the proverbial drowning person who will hold on to anything, even a serpent, to
survive. Zende's response again shows how bribery has become not only
a trade but also a culture which has infested everybody:

> I told you before that we were friends. I have been talking to him this
> evening as we were driving here; and he might just accept half a mil-
> lion. . . . And, you know, now that you have been appointed principal
> he is expecting a sizeable envelope. He now knows that you have
> everything to lose. (199)

It would appear the magistrate had a hand in Mikinding's appointment
as part of the bribery investment to place him in a vantage position to
hoodwink parents who bring their children to school for admission to
"buy" the few openings left for their children's admission. Indeed, we
would call this a cyclical culture investment, because Minkindong will
recoup this money and more from bribes received from parents for their
children's admission. That may inadvertently justify why today candi-
dates are willing to "buy" their admission into higher professional
schools in Cameroon such as ENAM (School of Administration and Ma-
gistracy), Social Work, Ecole Nornale (Higher Teachers' Training College), and CUSS (the college of medicine) at exorbitant costs because they
know it is an "investment." They will recover expenditure and the divi-
dends on graduation because their services, like the magistrate's and
police's, will be paid for by the clients in addition to their regular civil
service salaries. They will have to recover this money as soon as they
assume positions in public service, where citizens have to bribe to receive
services or have their children admitted into schools.

As the play ends, Mikindong exclaims, "The Magistrate! The Magistrate!" In fact, if the magistrate is corrupt, then who is free? The play ends
without telling us where Mikindong is going to come up with the money.
But it is common knowledge to assume that he will use his vantage
position as principal to extort money from parents who are willing to
"bid" for their children to be admitted into the high school. And the cycle
continues! It is therefore no surprise that for three consecutive years
(1998, 1999, and 2000), *Transparency International* placed Cameroon at the
top of the list of the most corrupt nations in the world. [17]

As the plays reveal, one of the legacies left by colonialism in Africa
and particularly in Cameroon is the creation of the culture of corruption.
Those entrusted with the responsibility of assuring justice and the protection of people's rights and property have become experts in the game of
corruption and bribery. Zende, Minkindong's Attorney and the magistrate's friend and accomplice in bribery and corruption and a very good

student of practical philosophy, attests to this hopeless and helpless situation in vivid terms:

> Until a revolution takes place, we will continue to function through the telephone call from above and the envelope from below, as . . . the policeman put it. (199)

The hope for the society lies in violent overthrow of the corrupt system. However, this violent overthrow does not guarantee freedom from corruption and bribery and the abuse of power, until the African undergoes a radical moral transformation. Emmanuel Dongala's *Johnny Mad Dog* (2002) tells the story where such attempts to overthrow the corrupt systems led to more corruption and brutality, transforming a war to right a wrong into one of ethnic cleansing and the replacement of one ruling tribe by another tribe. This indeed is a failed revolution like what Franz Fanon witnessed in Algeria and in other African countries where the white elites were replaced by African elites who were worse colonizers of their own kin than their colonial masters. That is why Albino in *The Dance of the Vampire* regrets that the local king is feeding on the blood of his citizens.

Butake's concern with corruption is a sort of continuation of Musinga's fight in *The Tragedy of Mr. No-Balance* (1976),[18] written much earlier than *Lake God* and *The Rape of Michelle*. *The Tragedy of Mr. No-Balance* goes much further to explain the driving forces that go to build the culture of corruption in the society. There is the dire need to imitate the colonial bourgeois lifestyle which is reflected in material acquisition such as the ownership of a car, a houseboy to please a girlfriend and expensive clothing. Mr. Zacharias Kongmelina No-Balance is a young, half-educated chief clerk with Vemsarbatreborp whose desire to impress his concubine, Mbarama, leads him into devilish, ingenious, and ruthless execution of corruption. His meager salary cannot sustain his image of a good lifestyle concomitant with his inflated or bloated image of an office clerk. He does not only want to imitate the lifestyle of his expatriate boss, but he also wants to usurp his boss's position. In his attempt to fill a vacant office position, he puts a price tag on it so that the highest bidder, irrespective of the bidder's credentials, will have the position. As the play opens, he complains that his concubine has not prepared the table for him. The concubine complains that she could not set his table because she cut her finger in the process of preparing food. In fact, she alludes to the fact that they need a houseboy to cook for them. To this Mr. No-Balance replies:

> Mbarama, I see no reason in that, for your not preparing me, at least, something to keep up my fast deflating sack. Moreover, you know for certain that my salary at present doesn't suffice to our fullest—I mean to have a car, a servant and some other pleasures Darling, just take it easy. (1)

They are interrupted by the entrance of Mr. No-Balance's friend Ernest, who announces that he is now "the proud owner of a Mercedes-Benz car." In response to this good news, Mr. No-Balance inquires from his friend:

> Now Ernest, let's come back to our good old days and talk matters over nicely. It's a secret I wish you to disclose to me. First, how did you come about your fortune; secondly, what help can you render my securing mine within the week? (2)

It is very obvious that Mr. No-Balance is looking for other unorthodox means to buy a car. He would not listen to Ernest's advice that his secret is "be honest, be fair in your dealings with men, and success is always at your door." Mr. No-Balance dismisses his friend's advice because he is hard pressed by time to satisfy his concubine with material things, in spite of his meager salary. Shortly after, he confides in his concubine his ingenious plan of corruption:

> No-Balance: Darling, life in abundance is come! You'll, any hour from now, start getting all the comforts you need. . . . You know . . . that I'm the Chief Clerk of our Corporation. But for the Manager, I'm second to none. At present, we've no office boy and this slows down the working of the office. Now, I'll importune the Manager to allow me advertise for the post of the office boy. I'm dead sure with unemployment in prevalence here, 100l will apply. I'll then ask them to give me some money, by the by, to attend a test. He who gives me the highest amount, gets the job, irrespective of his performance in the test. And this done and finished with, there'll be money, money all the way! (3)

With this plan in mind, he sets out to recruit an office boy. First, he clears the office of other occupants to create an atmosphere conducive to bribery, since bribery is a culture of intimate privacy. He spaces out the interview times so as accentuate the element of privacy. Furthermore, he uses the language of bribery such as "oiling of lips," throwing water up," and "dash" (gifts) to extort money from the applicants. In the end, he employs Bih, the least qualified who was fast enough to understand the language of corruption. But her employment is short-lived because her clumsiness, sloppiness, and illiteracy all betray her unsuitability for the job. As Mr. No-Balance's boss fires her, Bih resorts to the court of justice to recover the money she had bribed Mr. No-Balance with to have the job. To entrap him, the judicial system uses still another beautiful lady for whom Mr. No-Balance falls. To impress the lady, Mr. No-Balance inadvertently reveals how he had defrauded Bih of her cash for the job, though Bih was the least qualified for the job. The play ends with Mr. No-Balance being sentenced to "seventeen years' imprisonment with hard labour" (42). In his case, justice has triumphed over corruption and bribery. Women and a colonial lifestyle have beaten Mr. No-Balance into destruction. His society, unlike that of *The Rape of Michelle*, is one where the integrity of the police and the judicial system still reigns. His fall is not a norm because bribery and corruption still operate with impunity. Only the unfortunate ones like Mr. No-Balance are apprehended.

In *Lake God*, it is, in fact, the revolution that overthrows Fon Joseph, the colonial stooge. The villagers are much more politically astute and mature when they reject the Fon who, in a way, is part of the legacy left behind by colonialism. In the village, there is greater room for unity: the women are much more united and speak with one voice. The women, in fact, constitute in Ngugi's vision, "the forces that are pledged to conform our humanity, those whose aim is to open our eyes, to make us see tomorrow, asking ourselves about the future of our children" (53).[19] But in the city, everybody cares only about what affects him or her as an individual. Again, Ngugi would refer to them as "those who wish to lull us into closing our eyes, encouraging us to care only for our stomachs, without thinking about our country" (53). Butake's *Lake God*, therefore, stands in counterpoint to *The Rape of Michelle* in political maturity and clairvoyance. The city dwellers have a lot to learn from the illiterate but very politically sensitive and mature villagers of Ewawa. Colonialism and corruption are therefore twin evils that Cameroonians and, by extension, Africans must combat and defeat.

Stryker and Ndegwa see Africa's development crisis as "an apocalyptic amalgam of economic decline, human distress, recurrent famine, tyranny, and incessant civil wars and corruption" (390–91).[20] To this Butake adds neocolonialism or what we could term the colonial legacy of corruption. The only hope for Africa lies in the recent move toward political liberalization and democratization, much of it driven by Africans themselves in demanding accountability from their governments. And Butake's and Musinga's plays are written against this backdrop. The parallels between the contents of the plays and what is actually transpiring in some of the African countries are so obvious that we cannot miss the playwrights' political messages.

NOTES

1. Vincent B. Kyapoya, *The African Experience: An Introduction.* 2nd Edition (Upper Saddle River, NJ: Prentice Hall, 1998).

2. Joseph E. Harris, *Africans and Their History.* 2nd Edition (New York: Meridian, 1998).

3. Jean-Paul Sartre, Introduction. *The Colonizer and the Colonized.* By Albert Memmi (Boston: Beacon Press, 1967), xxiv.

4. Franz Fanon, *Black Skin, White Masks* (New York: Grove Press, 1952) and *The Wretched of the Earth* (New York: Grove Press, 1968).

5. Emmanuel N. Obiechina, *Language and Theme: Essays on African Literature* (Washington, D.C.: Howard University Press, 1990), 68.

6. Obiechina, 69.

7. Bole Butake, *Lake God and Other Places* (Yaoundé, Cameroon: Edition Cle, 1999). All references to any of Butake's plays shall be taken from this collection of plays and cited parenthetically.

8. Molefi Kete Asante, *Facing South to Africa: Toward an Afrocentric Critical Orientation* (Lanham, MD: Lexington Books, 2014).

9. Edem Kodjo, *Africa Tomorrow*. Trans. E. B. Khan (New York: Continuum, 1987).

10. Joseph Takougang and Milton Krieger, *African State and Society in the 1990s: Cameroon's Political Crossroads* (Boulder, CO: Westview Press, 1998).

11. Albert Memmi, *The Colonizer and the Colonized* (Boston: Beacon Press, 1967), 91–92.

12. Frantz Fanon, *The Wretched of the Earth* (New York: Grove Press, 1968), 390–98.

13. Paul Bohannan and Philip Curtin, *Africa and Africans*. Fourth Edition (Prospect Heights, IL: Waveland Press, 1995), 8–9.

14. Albert Memmi, 71.

15. Frantz Fanon, Letter to the Resident Minister 1956. Search for New Forms of Culture. Ed. Jo G. Leadingham (Acton, Mass: Copley Custom Publishing Group, 1999), 387–89.

16. Justice Mbuh, Albert Mukong HRDG's letter to the Prime Minister of Cameroon: Email to SCNFORUM, April 11, 2001 (SCNCFORUM Re:[africadaily3] 04/11/01:5:47p.m.), 1–4.

17. Transparency International, "The 2001 Corruption Perception Index." http://www.gwdg.de/~uwvw/2001Data.html. Also see http://transparencyinternational.org.

18. Kwo Victor Elame Musinga, *The Tragedy of Mr. No Balance* (Bamenda, Cameroon: Langaa Research & Publishing CIG, 2008). References to the play will be taken from the 1985 edition.

19. Ngugi wa Thiong'o, *Devil on the Cross* (Nairobi, Kenya: Heinemann, 1982), 53.

20. Richard Stryker and Stephen N. Ndegwa, "The African Development Crisis." *Africa*. 3rd Edition. Eds. Phyllis Martin and Patrick O'Meara (Bloomington: Indiana University Press, 1995), 375–94.

SIX

Female Empowerment and Political Change

Lake God, The Survivors, *and* And Palm Wine Will Flow

Bole Butake's three plays *Lake God* (1986), *The Survivors* (1989), and *And Palm Wine Will Flow* (1990) were all written against the backdrop of rapacious and inhumane oppressions of the seemingly silent and marginalized masses of the fictionalized communities of the North West Region of the Republic of Cameroon, Africa. These plays treat, among other issues, the themes of corruption, tyranny, nepotism, and the rampant abuse of power. These themes are not new in African literature, but Butake's approach shifts the traditional responsibility of the fight for political liberation which has hitherto been the preserve of the men to women. The silent suffering masses come to rely almost solely on the women who take the leading role for their liberation. This sudden and unexpected resurgence of females on the political field and their overwhelming success is intriguing and new to an audience that has for a very long time minimized and relegated women to secondary and/or subsidiary roles.

One question that comes up several times in these plays is "Where are the men?" The men have been exiled, incarcerated, or totally emasculated. In *And Palm Wine Will Flow*, the male sacred society, the Kibaranko is stripped of its judicial powers, unmasked, and sent on exile. The males regain their posture only after the female leader Kwengong calls a general assembly and declares a revolution against the Fon. She declares: "He cannot be Fon. The women have decided. No more Fons in the land" and that "Only . . . the people will decide [who] the Fon will be and for how long. And the affairs of the land shall be decided by all the people in the

71

market" (111).[1] She, in effect, declares the overthrow of the dictatorship and the institution of a genuine democracy. Again, in *The Survivors*, it is Mboysi, the female survivor, who overpowers the police officer. Before shooting him, she says mockingly:

> If I die after killing you, I will be satisfied that I had my revenge. Now, this is the moment of truth. Man! Man! Come and see what a woman can do. All of you, come along and celebrate the victory of woman over Officer. Come along and celebrate your liberation. (84)

Throughout his plays, Butake tends to suggest that, in reality, women are born with extraordinary powers that have simply been submerged, if not totally stifled, by the male-oriented and chauvinistic society, a society that has conspired to put women in a subordinate or secondary position. Butake's plays, therefore, are eye openers to the people who have usually assigned the business of political liberation only to men. In fact, the women reveal the truth subsumed in the saying that "What a man can do, a woman can do even better," and also that women can succeed where men have failed. This position reminds us, though remotely, of the relevance of Aristophanes' *Lysistrata* in which the women use sexual deprivation to extract collaboration from their husbands to gain political change—the signing of the peace treaty. And looking at the history of failed governments and revolutions on the continent of Africa, Butake may be sending out a coded message to the natives to give women a chance in the struggle for liberation from dictatorship, corruption, tyranny, and nepotism that have come to be the mainstay of African governments. Butake's projection of the woman as liberator parallels Ngugi's in Kenya: both of them attempt to liberate the female from their traditional domain of household chores, caretakers, and sex objects to a higher plane of political activism and change.

To better understand Butake's contribution to the new image of the woman in Cameroon literature and, by extension, African literature, it will be proper to view Butake's female characters in the light of the portrait of other African/black female characters in literature. It is a given that most African societies and cultures are prefixed on the concept of the male being in charge. In a predominantly patriarchal society, the woman has no voice in the domain of politics and in political decisions that involve the entire community. In a recent study of the status of women in indigenous African societies, Niara Sudarkasa expressed that most of the writers tend to characterize "women in African societies as 'jural minors' for most of their lives, falling under the guardianship first of their fathers and then their husbands . . . and ascribing to men a better situation, a higher status," leaving the women "saddled with home and domesticity."[2]

However, the hitherto negative perception of women is now giving way to positive portrayals. This seems to be the case with Debbie Ogedemgebe in *Destination Biafra* (1994) who succeeds in her political mission into Biafra land only after she refuses to succumb to the shackles of marriage and the responsibilities of motherhood. Although Pauline Uwakweh casts Debbie Ogedemgebe in *Destination Biafra* and Meridian in Walker's *Meridian* in glowing recognition of women militancy and political assertiveness and successes,[3] their successes are invariably linked to a primary liberation from the crutches of marriage, as if to say none of them could have succeeded in the context of marriage. Victoria Ramiez imputes the subjugated image of the African woman, her "weakened . . . ability to engage in public, economic spheres to the impact of colonialism on the lives of African women."[4]

This might have been true in certain African societies and also in the past, but, as bell hooks accurately discusses in *Ain't I A Woman: Black Women and Feminism* (1981), we cannot form an accurate picture of women's status by simply calling attention to the roles assigned females under patriarchy.[5] Butake's women often operate not as isolated, mystical priestesses imbued with cultural or spiritual powers, or as women who only use their hidden powers when men are confused; they constitute a force, an entire group, with powers enough to effect profound and lasting sociopolitical changes in the set-up of an entire community, and, by extension, a nation. Their men are not only confused, but they have been rendered completely emasculated, powerless, and helpless.

Furthermore, Butake has no qualms portraying his heroines in feminine terms and characteristics: they are first and foremost women, young and old, married and/or unmarried, and those who are married are faithful to the institution of marriage and child-rearing, and acting in ways befitting their gender. Unlike other African writers, Butake does not argue for the women, nor does he let his heroines argue for their emancipation, but he portrays them the way they are: intelligent, politically conscious, militant, capable of taking charge of both the family and the larger unit—the community or the state. His women, therefore, operate at a level much higher than that intimated or studied by the above critics and authors, especially as evidenced by the isolated and individualized women of Achebe's novels. However, these women are not power-drunk or power-hungry, for they are humble enough to understand that power was meant to be used for the good of the society. Once they have succeeded in bringing order or positive change to a chaotic society, they step back and allow their men to assume the biblical role of the "head of the family." They step back into the roles and positions which they consider sacred and ennobling—motherhood. The women do not use their secret power to denigrate their husbands. The only warning they give to the men is that the men will be overthrown again if and when they fail to use political power for the good of all, that is, if the male heads of council revert to dictatorship and the abuse of power.

Butake is equally ahead of his time in moving courageously and treading against the prevailing gender war and stereotypes in revealing, without any excuses or excesses, the woman as heroine in a society where men fear to act or men have been stripped of their power to act. This conviction was probably borne out of the Takumbeng and Anlu Principles of the North West Region of Cameroon, with which Butake was very familiar, a phenomenon that casts women in fresh and more dynamic light, uplifting the heroism of women (married and unmarried) to greater heights. And this was to be the propelling point of Bole Butake's plays.

The Takumbeng and Anlu traditions in the North West Region of Cameroon consist of elderly, usually married, women who wield and exercise immense political power and leadership in the presence of issues of grave sociopolitical importance. In his discussion of its importance, Joseph Takougang and Milton Krieger maintain that this sacred society of women, born in Kom and eventually spread throughout Bamenda in the North West Region of Cameroon, manifested its tremendous powers in the state of emergency period when the main opposition political party leader and 145 others (one-third of them women) were confined in Ni Fru Ndi's residence in Ntarikon, Bamenda, following the uprising in protest of the results of the contested 1992 presidential election that declared Paul Biya winner. The core of the recent Takumbeng is, Takougang and Krieger assert, "the public, silent, but eloquent practice which brings post-menopausal women to disputed terrain with sacred grasses and other materials from nature, invoking maternal authority to restore peace, threatening and using bodily exposure against violators, whom it is meant to shame and stop."[6] Following up in the footsteps of the sacred and yet politically powerful Kom Anlu in the region, the practice gained sharper political focus and wider attention in the context of the political disturbances of the 1990s, particularly in the Northwest Region of Cameroon.

A week after the declaration of a state of emergency in the Northwest Region, the Takumbeng scored their most decisive victory over Cameroon's security forces when they challenged the Cameroon security forces in Bamenda, who attempted to block a protest march, for the release of members and sympathizers of the Social Democratic Front that had been arrested and incarcerated. They displayed traditional paraphernalia and postures of defiance to excessive authority, including disrobing, against very uncomfortable security forces. This open, though unarmed defiance, buttressed by cadets and party placards, was led by sixty Njinikom women who trekked over fifty miles to confront the Governor of the region in support of the incarcerated party leaders and sympathizers. This show of willpower culminated in the immediate and unconditional release of the village SDF officials by the governor. Clearly a localized experience and unmatched anywhere else, Takumbeng demonstrated the unleashed or hidden power of the women folk, thereby constituting a convergence zone within the female sociopolitical field of custom and innovation. The women achieved what their boys and husbands could not. They not only disarmed the security forces, but they unleashed the power of women to effect meaningful change in a society that badly needed that change, and which for long had undermined the ability of the women to engage in political discourse. And this action reminds us of Aristophanes' Greek women, under the leadership of Lysistrata in *Lysistrata* (411 BC) who deprived their lovers and husbands sexual privileges to extract collaboration for the negotiation of peace to end the Peloponnesian War. While Aristophanes used sex, Butake has added food as one of the strangleholds or power of women over men.

Butake's plays, therefore, dramatize in much more poignant and vivid terms the ferocity of the proverbial sleeping dogs. In *The Survivors, And Palm Wine Will Flow*, and *Lake God*, Butake portrays a society in which the women, phoenix-like, respond to the helplessness of the so-called "more noble sex" to assert their hitherto dormant political power and to effect change. In *The Survivors*, the woman's role is not an easy task as the heroine, Mboysi, must first succumb to the stereotypical role of woman as a sex object in order to put herself in a position to defeat the much dreaded and all-powerful, but corrupt, police officer. The ultimate liberalization of the survivors is attained when Mboysi tricks the officer who has exploited her sexually into giving her the gun with which she shoots him. In *And Palm Wine Will Flow*, the women take the action to a broader and much more political arena as they team up in defiance of their husbands to oust the tyrannical, ethnocentric and corrupt Fon from his palace in favor of a more democratic form of government whose leadership will henceforth be decided democratically by the people.

The actions of the women in effecting change attest to the point that Butake's plays are fundamentally concerned with moral choices. In this light, Butake seems to be asking the same questions the American playwright Arthur Miller asked:

> How may a man make of the outside world a home? How and in what ways must he struggle, what must he strive to change and overcome within himself and outside himself if he is to find the safety, the surroundings of love, the ease of soul, the sense of identity and honor which, evidently all men have connected with the idea of family?[7]

The answers to these fundamental questions are found in the various forms of revolts borne of a strong desire to overcome the corrupt and tyrannical leadership. This fight or struggle must be championed by selfless, wise, fearless, and determined citizens who are committed to change. In Butake's imagination, the men have lost their ability to raise these questions or find answers to them that will adequately address the political conditions that prevail. In *And Palm Wine Will Flow*, the initial revolt of the women begins with their coming to terms with their innate, though traditionally ignored, qualities. They have in-built powers, in addition to their primary responsibilities of providing sustenance to the entire family and community at large, which they could use to effect change in the community, to create a sense of dignity, identity, and honor. In fact, the women in a chorus challenge their husbands into action by revealing to them how "manless" they have become:

> Shey! Our husband!
> Father of our children!
> Shey, our husband! Are you sitting there quietly
> When our farms have been seized from us?
> What shall we eat? What shall our children eat?
> What shall you eat, Shey? We know you are in there.
> Speak up, Shey. Or shall we come into the sacred presence in
> Our present condition? Speak up, Shey! (95–96)

This challenge falls on deaf ears, as the men refuse to come out of hiding to stand up against the Fon who has seized their wives' farm lands and given them to "manless men like Kibanya [who] have their caps topped by red feather by the Fon himself" (96). In fact, Kwengong, the leader of the women, and all the other women are impatient with their husbands' lack of courage and heroism in the presence of this crisis. In this regard, Kwengong asks Shey, "how long shall we wait to see this judgement come? What shall we, your wives, do?" (97). The men's sacred society, traditionally empowered to resolve conflicts between the Fon and his subjects, has been emasculated. Even the Kibaranko has fallen; it would do nothing to restore the lands seized by the Fon. Shey is so helpless that Kwengong regrets and expresses this change in her nostalgic bewilderment:

> The times are changing, Shey. The times have changed. Look at you!
> What is your reward? After how many years of royal service to the
> gods and the land? The farmlands of your wives have been given to the
> wives of the lowliest of the low. . . Because he pays respect to the Fon.
> (97)

Shey Ngong's response is limited to speaking instead of taking action. He can only say sheepishly:

> Wife, I will not pay respect to a man who respects only palm-wine and
> food. When does the Fon really rule? How often has he consulted the
> council of elders or even implemented decisions by that revered body
> for the common good of all the land? (97)

And talking about the Fon, Shey Ngong remarks regrettably: "As soon as he smelt, tasted and felt power, he turned against me" (106), and Tapper, on his part, reports that "The Fon has seized the palm-bush. His watchdogs are there now. They beat me severely. My clothes are tatters" and that, "only women are singing, the whole land is full of women, not a single man is left" (107). Tapper's statement virtually summarizes the idea about the transvaluation of values: the women have now become "men," and the men who have taken to silence, hiding, or verbal threats have become "women." It is important to note Tapper's use of the word "women," which operates on two levels. There is the traditional belief in women as a gender well suited for raising praises in honor of the Fon and giving birth to children. They are gifted with angelic voices to do so, and they own that domain. However, when men revert to singing in praise of the Fon, they trade their manliness for womanliness. That is why there is constant reference to the absence of men, not because the male gender is not there; rather the men have mortgaged their male militancy for a subservience which was always reserved for women. This explains why Kwengong's rise to power is unprecedented. She, like Lady Macbeth in Shakespeare's *Macbeth,* "unsexes" herself and assumes the male gender attributes in order to energize and spur the society to action.

Kwengong declares war against the all-powerful Fon in the war song "The sun of the land has set! The elephant has fallen! The lion of Ewawa is no more!" She promises that the Fon will not escape "the wrath of the women" (108). She tells Shey Ngong that the women have "decided to take very drastic action against the desecration of the gods and the ancestors" (109). She invokes and assumes the posture of the "Earth-goddess [who] needs no one's leave—To walk where her feet will" (109). She challenges the Fon who still holds to the patriarchal belief that women are powerless. The exchange between the Fon and Kwengong portrays in vivid terms this tension between the ruler and the ruled and the eventual victory of the women over the Fon and, by extension, over the men:

> Fon: Watch your tongue, woman Earth-goddess indeed! Your wretched husband . . . is still smarting from the venom of my power and you dare to insult our royal presence by profanely pronouncing our sacred name?

> Kwengong: The only husband Earth-goddess honors Chila Kintasi
> Is the whole of Ewawa. Here [urine] are the wares the women commanded deliverance to their Fon. May they make you call another feast before the sun goes to sleep.

> Fon: Urine! Urine! What is the meaning of this abomination?

> Kwengong: Not urine, Chila Kintasi,
> But the savoury juice from
> The vaginas of those upon whom
> You wield power, Fon . . . .
> Drink the liquor from the vaginas
> And feel the power of power

> Fon: I will die first.

> Kwengong: Then you will die indeed, Chila Kintasi.

Die and deliver the land from the
Abominations of drunkenness and gluttony!
Die! Chila Kintasi, die!
And save the land from merry-making!
Die, Fon! So that we may think!
The people need your death to think!
Die! Die! Die! (109–10)

The above exchange brings out two very crucial and irrefutable new pictures of women: they have awakened to their own strength by overcoming the traditional notion of powerlessness that was formerly ascribed to them; they have realized and used the idea that the liberation of their land resides in their own hands. Hence, they refer to their power as the "power of power," the earth goddesses who have control over life as the givers and takers of life.

Throughout the play, the men do not have the audacity to confront their Fon. They either only talk about him at his back, or his supporters "adulate him" (102), because the men who attempt to oppose him "disappear," that is, "they are taken to Ekpang . . . And killed" (103). The fear of Ekpang (the modern equivalence of the political prisons in Kondegue, Yaoundé) has reduced the men to cowards and puppets of the tyrannical and corrupt Fon (president), who has pushed aside and stripped the council of elders (the National Assembly) of their vested powers to rule the people. He now rules on his own terms.

As a result, Kwengong declares the overthrow of a dictatorship, an autocracy, saying: "They [women] have decided. No more Fons in the land!" And to Tapper's question, "So what will happen?" her response is emphatic and definitive: "The people will rule through the council of elders led by Shey, here. The day he takes the wrong decision, that same day, the people shall meet in the market place and put another at the head of the Council of elders" (113). Kwengong understands and respects the traditional role of men in this society, and the women are humble and unpresumptive enough to relegate "rulership" to the men, while holding to the real power—that of impeachment in the case of male abuse of the political power. Neither do the women use their power to subjugate men or to continuously remind them of that loss of their "manliness." There is a silent and understood understanding of who holds the power and who runs the society. It is at this point that the men become galvanized to join the victory chorus. Shey Ngong comes out of hiding to declare the triumph of democracy over dictatorship:

We must break clean from the past. Take the sacred gong of Nyombom and let it resound in all the nooks and corners of the land. From today, this bugle will stay here in the sacred grove, a living symbol of our enslavement by the Fon and his notables. Take the sacred gong to the people and let its sound vibrate through their very souls, a symbol of their liberation. (114)

The play ends with the chanting of the song of liberation, given the demise of the Fon, led by Tapper:

> People of Ewawa!
> People of this land!
> As the sun rises at dawn
> So shall we all meet
> In the market place
> To decide on the destiny of this land
> No more shall we allow
> One person to rule our land for us!
> From this moment, palm-wine shall no longer flow
> In this land of Ewawa. (114)

Although the final lines of the play are given to the men, it is crucial to note that it is the women who fought and won the battle of "liberation." The men are simply second-class partakers of the fallouts of the struggle. The women are conscious of the fact that they must recapture and relinquish the "manhood" of their husbands to them, after having made the cogent point that theirs was the "power of power" (110). The men are, therefore, the proverbial empty vessels that make a lot of noise, while the silent women are the veritable sources power.

The women's remarkable achievement in *And Palm Wine Will Flow* is equally matched by Mboysi's in *The Survivors*. In an attempt to find sustenance after a devastating natural disaster, five survivors (Old One, Tata, Bolame, Mboysi, (the lone adult female) and Ngujoh) approach a relief camp set up by the national government with contributions from foreign donors to provide free food, clothes, and shelter to the victims of the disaster. This camp is headed by a corrupt military officer from the national army whose sole duty is to oversee the peaceful and equitable distribution of the materials to the unfortunate victims of the disaster. Unfortunately, Officer transforms the camp into a trading post, from which he enriches himself and extorts sexual favors from those female victims who come for the goods. As the children start crying of hunger and thirst, Ngujoh and the young boy Tata go down the valley to search for water. At their first encounter with the officer, Ngujoh, the mature male retreats, is overcome by fear, and then collapses. The Old One, who, by virtue of his gender and age, is supposed to protect the survivors, challenges the officer in martial, patriarchal terms: "Who are you, hiding your face in the bush like the coward you are, uttering menaces and pointing things (gun) at people? If you're a man, show your face and talk to me. Man to man!" (62).

Old One's challenge here again is borne out of the stereotypical concept that only men can and ought to be engaged in martial activities, and that the survival of the family lies solely in the hands of the males. Soon the men realize that they are powerless to confront a police officer who has a gun. However, when Ngujoh intimates that Mboysi negotiate with Officer on the basis of her education, we begin to see a shift in power paradigm. Incidentally, it is Mboysi, the female who has both sorts of power to appease and disarm Officer—education and sex:

> Ngujoh: We can get him to negotiate. With [Mboysi's] cooperation.
>
> Mboysi: What do you mean? With my co-operation?
>
> Ngujoh: You speak to him in the language he understands, having been a teacher at our school. Moreover, you're a woman with great charms.
>
> Old One: Oh hoo! A woman will soften the hardest heart.
>
> Ngujoh: Especially the heart of Officer. (63–64)

In fact, Old One and Ngujoh assert, though ironically, that the woman has unfathomable sacred powers at her disposal to use in times of crisis. Mboysi's literacy and "great charms" become stronger weapons than guns in the fight for survival. Mboysi is no Lady Macbeth in terms of political astuteness and hunger for power, but she has the demagogic connivance of a Lady Macbeth as she endears herself to Officer through sexual favors. But she is no fool, as she studies her way into the comfort zone of Officer. But before she "sells" herself to Officer for food, water, and clothes, she asks the men a very critical question about Officer: "How do I ask him? If you, men, have failed to convince another man, can a poor woman do?" (64). Old One regrets that things have changed and that the old values have given way to the new. This change in roles comes out clearly in the dialogue between Old One and Ngujoh:

> Old One: I see. In our times problems were resolved by men. Men discussed and, as you put it, negotiated with other men. Man to man. But today, I am learning something new I now know that Officer prefers to discuss and negotiate with . . .
>
> Ngujoh: Never mind your times, Old One. Those days were ancient days. Today, women are the key to power. Even the door with seven locks on it can be unlocked by a woman. In your days you used reason. And only when reason failed did you fall back on combat.
>
> Old One: Those were the days, indeed. Man to man. Word against word. Fist for fist. Those were the days! (65)

As Mboysi succeeds in bringing food, water, and life back to the survivors, Ngujoh, who is disgusted with the airs Mboysi is putting up, questions such effrontery: "When did women start talking like that in the presence of men?" to which Old One replies, "You sent her to Officer, didn't you?" (70). Ngujoh therefore has to contend himself with the fact that, ". . . this woman has power over us" and Old One reminds him that "this woman has power over Officer. With her help Officer will allow us to go to Ewawa" (70). Officer himself echoes Old One, telling Mboysi that the people's survival depends on her: "They can wait. Their survival depends on you. . . . No one cares if they survive. Without you, I don't care about their survival" (73).

At the climax of the play, Mboysi has come to the realization that she has to reduce herself to a prostitute to save her people. She must now make a moral choice between, on the one hand, wallowing in prostitution to save her people and, on the other, regaining her self-pride and dignity through starvation and death. She sees the clothes Officer gave her as "the prize of my disgrace," and confronts Ngujoh for having sold her into prostitution: "It was you who sent me to him, not so? You will pay for it now. Now! I say, you will pay for it now! You manless man!" (78). Proverbially, the men have lost what it takes to be men and have traded that "manness' with Mboysi who will become and act the "man" and face the Officer "man to man," to use Old One's words to Officer (62).

Mboysi then metamorphosizes into a "man" to face her adversary, Officer: "I will show Officer that in spite of his gun and loud menaces, he is only a man, a mortal" (79). After all, Mboysi has just proven that men are no longer men and that they are not invincible; they have become "manless," and Officer is no exception. Old One recognizes this truth as he remarks to Ngujoh about Mboysi's "manness:" "Between you and that woman, I do not know who the man is" (79). Officer himself confesses and succumbs to the power Mboysi has over him as he says: "Woman has power over Officer. My heart is soft because of you, woman" (83). Mboysi uses her pretext of ignorance about guns to take the gun away from Officer. Now with her literacy, feminine charm, and the gun in her hand, Mboysi exercises absolute control over Officer and all the men. She points the gun at Officer to get his confession on corruption, sexual harassment, and public theft:

> Your generosity, indeed, Officer! Tell me more. How much have you carried away for yourself and those who order you from above . . . How much you have looted and hidden away . . . This is the moment of truth. The moment of your death and the moment of our liberation . . . Keep crawling, you rotten maggot! Even if I die after killing you, I will be satisfied that I had my revenge. Now, this is the moment of truth. . . Man! Man! Come and see what a woman can do. All of you, come along and celebrate the victory of woman over Officer. Come along, all of you and celebrate your liberation.
> The elephant has fallen!
> The elephant has fallen!
> The lion is no more
> Woman is great! (83–84)

Toward the end of the play, Mboysi shoots Officer, but she is, in turn, shot by another officer who has come to relieve the fallen officer. Her killing of Officer is tantamount to the victory, determination and courage

over injustice, harassment, and the abuse of power. It is equally a symbolic blow for justice and liberation. Her act is a model, a shift in power
paradigm for all the Ewawas and the Cameroonians at large who have
been cornered by powerlessness, passivity, and poverty to wake up and
fight for their dignity. Mboysi's struggle is a struggle for some measure of
dignity through self-sacrifice, determination, and commitment to a noble
course of action. Indeed, unlike in Jimmy Porter's days in *Look Back in
Anger*, Mboysi's death is a historic statement that there are still noble
causes to fight for. Unfortunately, the new Officer looks at Mboysi's
corpse still in sexist terms: "What a beautiful body to waste! Strange!
Strange! . . . [a] casualty" (85). She is not referred to as a human, but as
material waste of a sexual object—a beautiful body. In the reader's mind,
she has risen from the level of a victim (a casualty) to a hero—a leader of
the lost. What greater love did somebody show than to lay her life down
for her people, so that her people will be saved!

What *The Survivors* and *And Palm Wine Will Flow* make clear is that the
words and chorus of liberation are sung by women, not men. Although
Mboysi pays with her life, her soul sings the song of freedom. Freedom
has never been given on a platter, but it has always been fought for. In
these plays, Butake sounds a very prophetic note by telling the Ewawa
people and, by extension, her society that the present times are the best
for change and that they must take off their cloak of gender chauvinism
and give the Takumbeng (the women sacred society) a chance at change.
Traditionally, most Ewawa women do not get drunk with wine. Therefore, they tend to retain their sanity, and it is about time the drunk rulers
who barricade themselves in the palaces with fellow drunkards and hand
clappers stepped aside for these women to run their societies, albeit
through appointed leaders who are subject to the people's will and ideas.

In the Ewawa society, for over forty years now, palm-wine flowed
and the hand-clapping legislature fed fat on the wealth of the nation like
"maggots." However, it is time for the Mboysis, the Kwengongs, and the
Takumbeng who have the "power of power" to exercise this power to
bring sanity to the nation. It is a moral choice between letting things
remain the way they have always been, as the men do, or standing up
against tyranny by sacrificing their lives (as Mboysi does) to change the
course of history.

In the two plays, the men are completely aware of the fact that the
nation is in dire need of change of leadership, but they have been inca-
pacitated by the all-powerful but still vulnerable Lion of Ewawa, Fon, or
Officer. The struggle for liberation can only be sustained and ultimately
attained through a concerted stand against the tyranny that threatens to
undercut their cultural roots and traditions. The women in *The Survivors*
and *And Palm Wine Will Flow* live out the principle that there are still
noble causes worth fighting for. In fact, Ngugi in his *Devil On the Cross*
addresses the dilemma of the Kenyans in a way that resonates with the

Cameroonian folk, especially as both artists (Kenyan Ngugi and Cameroonian Butake) share a common sense of history:

> Our lives are a battlefield on which is fought a continuous war between the forces that are pledged to confirm our humanity and those determined to dismantle it; those whose aim is to open our eyes, to make us see the light and look to tomorrow, asking ourselves about the future of our children, and those who wish to lull us into closing our eyes, encouraging us to care only for our stomachs today, without thinking about the tomorrow of our country.[8]

In both *The Survivors* and *And Palm Wine Will Flow*, the police officers and the Fon and his red feathered hand-clappers respectively align with the dismantlers, who lull the natives into closing their eyes to the abuse of power and corruption, encouraging them to care only for their stomachs. That is why palm-wine keeps on flowing. The officer in *The Survivors*, who feeds maggot-like on the misfortunes of the survivors, plays the same role. In the opposite camp, we see the women who think about their families and the welfare of the commonwealth, who stand up against the tyrants because they are "pledged to confirm our humanity." They are poised to regain the atmosphere of peace and sanity of the Council of Elders that used to exist, but the temptation is that as soon as that happens, those who smell power will likely abuse it. That was the Fon's history, but this time the women are there to watch the new leader.

Similarly, in *Lake God*, the women rise up against their Fon for condoning the destruction of their crops by the cattle. While it is true that farming is almost the sole preoccupation of the women, the crisis caused by the destruction of the crops would normally cause the women to look up to their husbands to resolve the situation. Tanto alludes to this when he says:

> This is an emergency, and there are still men in the land. Kwifon will forget the crimes of the Fon in order to save the land. I will get the seven pillars of Kwifon and they will put their heads together. They will meet here since they can no longer gain access to their sanctuary in the palace. (22–23)

In response to Tanto, Shey Bo-Nyo affirms that: "There are still men in the land. It might still be saved" (23). The exchange between the two men points to two very cardinal issues: the men have a very essential role or even the primary role to play in resolving crises; secondly, however, the men have been stripped of their sacred power by being barred "access to their sanctuary in the palace." Hence, Tanto's and Shey Bo-Nyo's declarations are impotent as they are issued from a position of weakness. Instead of the male war society, the Kwifon, taking the lead, it is the women's Fibuen and its adherents who take up the war song against the Fon. In fact, the stage directions capture this situation vividly:

> There is a crowd of women in the village square. After the abortive
> encounter with the Fon, and because of the fever of the Fibuen, [the
> women] display a spirit of defiance that would shock their men folk.
> Something like mob action in which the women have no inhibitions.
> When action begins, there is the sound of the now familiar horn of
> Fibuen followed by an exhilarating ululation. (24)

This is immediately followed by the celebration of victory in a song led
by another woman Yensi:

> I lack words with which to express my joy. The happiness that is in my
> heart cannot be shown on my face. The happenings of today have
> shown that, in spite of what some people say, the ways of the land are
> alive. We must be one person to succeed in our present undertaking.
> We must be one woman. Some here have only recently been given into
> marriage. Their bellies are hot. There are others who cannot control
> their emotions of love and sympathy. There are still others who will
> easily succumb to threats and the fear of being beaten. You all know
> where we have built the sanctuary of the Fibuen . . . The sanctuary is
> the refuge for those without a heart. Go there if you cannot look your
> man in the face and tell him to go eat shit. (24)

The women then take the "oath of sealed lips" in rebellion against their
husbands. In addition, they decide not to go to bed with or to give food to
their husbands, moving a step higher than the women in Aristophanes'
Lysistrata who only refused sexual privileges to their husbands and lovers until the peace treaty was signed. Here, we find the women breaking
loose of their traditional status of sexual condescension and managers of
household chores of cooking for and feeding their husbands. In fact, they
turn their supposed weaknesses to strength. The vacuum created by the
exiled male Kwifon (39, 41) is filled now by the women's Fibuen. Fisiy,
one of the notables, quickly acknowledges the importance of women in
response to Forgwei's challenge to female political activism: "Who gave
such powers to women? We cannot really blame the women. The Fon is
the one breaking the laws and destroying the land in the name of this
new religion brought by Father Leo" (30).

The overthrow of the men and the Fon by women in defense of their
land enhances and reflects Jodi Jacobson's assessment of women's contribution to development in the developing world. It is as if women were
reacting to Jacobson's article, "Closing the Gender Gap in Development,"
in which he argues that women perform the lion's share of work in subsistence economies, toiling longer hours and contributing to family in-
come than men do. Yet in a world where economic value is computed in
monetary terms alone, women's work is not counted as economically
productive when money changes hands. Women are viewed as "unproductive" by government statisticians, economists . . . and even by their
husbands. A huge proportion of the world's real productivity therefore

remains undervalued, and women's essential contributions to the welfare of families and nations remain unrecognized.[9]

Jacobson's assertion justifies why Butake's men are very reluctant to accept the fact that the women folk can rise up against them and their Fon. On the other hand, the plays reveal how far Butake is ahead of his contemporaries in depicting a new woman, one who could rise out of the ashes of the past into a position of imminence. The woman has always been there, but she has never been given the freedom to be her true self, to exercise some of the power embodied in her person. She has often been told to stay off politics and "men's" domain and activities. However, in Butake's plays, their fight is both spiritual/sacred and political. In *Lake God*, the women's fight to regain their land is a sacred duty because, as Alan Durning maintains, "the sustainable use of local resources is simple self-preservation for people whose way of life is tied to the fertility and natural abundance of the land" and who are "bound to their land through relationships [that are] both practical and spiritual, routine and historical."[10]

In short, these plays have displayed the hidden powers of women in the search for peace and political change, a fight in which women take a leading role. This change in power paradigm is swift and unexpected, catching the men by surprise because nobody ever envisioned a situation where and when the women could be so courageous as to challenge the male status quo and leadership. They do not only challenge the status quo, but succeed in bringing lasting change to a society very much in need of change. This may be a herald to future roles of women in politics, but this tactical victory by women is handled in such a subtle way as not to create further battles of the sexes. Butake allows women to retreat to the comfort of their homes, while leaving their husbands to rule or run the society. But this time, the women make it very clear that they will wake up and retake this power if the men attempt to revert to the period of corruption, anarchy, and dictatorship. The women now become the watchdogs over the male-dominated leadership. However, they do not provoke or humiliate the men with the victory they have won—they are humble, not self-conceited, and are pleased to gain back a peaceful environment where they can continue to live and perform their familial responsibilities without inhibitions or harassment.

NOTES

1. Bole Butake, *Lake God and Other Plays* (Yaoundé: Editions CLE, 1999) 111. Further references to Butake's plays shall be taken from this edition and shall be cited in parenthesis henceforth in this chapter.

2. Niara Sudarkasa, "The 'Status of Women' in Indigenous African Societies." *Women in Africa and the African Diaspora.* Eds. Rosalyn Terborg-Penn, Sharon Harley, and Andrea B. Rushing (Washington, D.C.: Howard University Press, 1987), 25.

3. Pauline Ada Uwakweh, "Female Choices: The Militant Option in Buchi Emecheta's Destination Biafra and Alice Walker's Meridian." *Nwanyibu: Womanbeing and African Literature*. Vol. 1. Eds. Egejuru and Katrak, 10–15.

4. Victoria Ramiez, "The Impact of Colonialism on African Women's lives in Novels by Marian Ba, Buchi Emecheta, and Ama Ata Aidoo." SIRAS (Frankfort, Kentucky, April 12, 2000), 144–49.

5. bell hooks, *Ain't I A Woman: Black Women and Feminism* (Boston, MA: South End Press, 1992), 12.

6. Joseph Takougang and Milton Krieger, *The African State and Society in the 1990s: Cameroon's Political Crossroads* (Boulder, CO: Westview Press, 1998), 232–33.

7. Arthur Miller, "The Family in Modern Drama." *The Theater Essays of Arthur Miller*. Eds. Robert A Martin and Steven R. Centola (New York: Da Capo Press, 1996), 73.

8. Ngugi wa Thiong'o, Devil On the Cross (London: Heinemann, 1982), 53.

9. Jodi Jacobson, "Closing the Gender Gap in Development." *State of the World: A World Watch Institute Report on Progress Toward a Sustainable Society*. Ed. Linda Starke. (New York: W. W. Norton & Company, 1993), 61–62.

10. Alan Durning, "Supporting Indigenous Peoples." *State of the World*. Ed. Linda Starke, 85–91.

SEVEN

Symbol and Meaning in *Lake God and Other Plays*

The human and material toll of the explosion of Lake Nyos in Cameroon on August 21, 1986 generated heated discussions about the circumstances of this cataclysmic event. Interestingly, this situation would be of cardinal importance to Bole Butake; a seminal experience that runs through his plays as he analyzes local, traditional, and governmental reactions to this catastrophe. In the foreword to his collection of plays, Butake states that he uses theater as an informal tool of awakening and conscientizing people in areas such as female empowerment, land use management, democracy, human rights and citizenship, good management of community property, environmental protection, and socioeconomic uplift.[1] He generally relies on symbols such as the *Fibuen, Kwifon,* and cattle in *Lake God;* Officer in *The Survivors; kibaranko* in *And Palm Wine Will Flow;* shoes in *Shoes and Four Men in Arms;* and vampires in *Dance of the Vampires* as vehicles of transmitting his ideas. We shall argue in this chapter that these symbols are fundamental in Butakean drama because they generally illustrate, on the one hand, dominant and dominated groups of society, and, on the other, Butake's vision of ending the oppression and exploitation of the destitute majority by a vicious minority.

According to Northrop Frye, a symbol often implies at least two things: A, the symbol proper, and B, the thing represented or symbolized by it. At times, it is important to approach literature centrifugally, paying attention to external sources if we are to make factual significance out of it.[2] In fact, place, time, or the individual appreciating a sign are important in attributing an aesthetic function to it. C. S. Peirce, the founder of semiotics, identified three kinds of signs. The "iconic," where the sign somehow resembles what it represents such as the photograph of a person; the "indexical," whereby the sign is associated with what it is a sign of, for example, smoke with fire; and the "symbolic," where the sign is arbitrarily or conventionally associated with its referent. Semiotics groups these categorizations into two basic classes, that is, denotation, or what the sign stands for, and connotation, or other signs associated with it. There are general principles of representation that give rise to valid inference which itself is a kind of symbolization.[3] In a work of art, a sign may have a contextual meaning or historical symbolism. Therefore, meaning in a text is not restrictive, but takes into consideration other texts, codes, and ethos in literature and society. The study of symbolism in Butake's plays is informed by Frye's and Peirce's definitions of a symbol. In addition, an understanding of the symbols in Butake's drama necessitates knowledge of the cultural and historical background of his works.

The play *Lake God* is the story of a recalcitrant Fon who refuses to perform sacrifices on behalf of his people because of his newfangled Christianity. Encouraged by the overbearing Father Leo, Fon Joseph Kimbong turns his back on tradition thereby provoking the wrath of the lake god against the clan. This obstinate Fon owns most of the cattle in the land and an angry group of women protests before him against the destruction of crops by cows. They want him to either stop the encroachment of cattle on agricultural land, or chase away graziers like Dewa. By acting together as the *Fibuen*, these women emphasize the preservation of a distinctive order in which community well-being is their chief concern.[4]

The *Fibuen*, or women's cult, usually convenes for a range of reasons, including fertility issues, funeral ceremonies, title taking, judicial functions, and defense in warfare.[5] It is often made up of elderly women who sometimes even march nude to protest against unpopular decisions taken by leaders or deviant practices in society. This group is similar to the *Takumbeng* (elderly women) who scored a decisive victory over Cameroon's security forces immediately after the declaration of a state of emergence in the North West Region of Cameroon in 1992. The *Takumbeng* prevented security forces from aborting a protest march by sympathizers of the Social Democratic Front (SDF) for the release of incarcerated supporters of this opposition party. Just like the *Takumbeng*, the *Fibuen* in *Lake God* are complaining about leadership and the passive or colluding attitude of the Fon toward their suffering. Once these women of the *Fibuen* appear in public, there is consternation as noted in the anguish of Doggo and Kinchin: "They are coming, Mbe! They are coming! / Mbe! The women! A whole crowd of them!" (12). So awe-inspiring is this group of women that they often leave the beholder dumbfounded: "What my eyes have seen, my mouth cannot speak, Mbe!" (12), says the frightened Doggo.

The *Fibuen* could be seen as the moral authority of the land, checking against the abuse of power by the Fon who not only refuses to perform annual sacrifices to the lake god, but also is responsible for the destruction of crops by cattle. Under the leadership of Ma Kusham, the *Fibuen* performs the oath of sealed lips, which involves the sprinkling of some liquid on the women while enjoining them to secrecy concerning any collective action that they may embrace in order that the Fon listen to their grievances. Punishment for violating this oath of secrecy, as stated by Ma Kusham, could be drastic: "if my mouth discloses what my ears have heard in this gathering, may my tongue swell and fill my mouth with dumbness" (25). As a result, the women agree to starve their husbands of sex and food until they support their decision of driving away graziers and cattle from the land. By undertaking this task, these women, as John Nkemngong Nkengasong avers in his essay "Butake and Aristophanes: Libidinal Strategies and the Politics of the Traditional Woman," are portrayed as having a high sense of commitment, imbued with uncanny bravery and unity of purpose.[6]

Central to the conflict between the Fon and the women is the question of cattle. Indeed, cattle are a symbol of the exploitation of the poor by the affluent. In this regard, Dewa colludes with the Fon to rob the women of agricultural yield: "All the women who have farms in Ngangba will starve this year. Dewa's cattle have ruined all the corn" (15), laments Nkfusai. Regrettably, Dewa appears to be above the law and he is aware that the women cannot harm him because he connives with the Fon: "And when we went to his kiban to demand an explanation, he laughed in our face and told us to take him to the highest court in the land" (15), recounts Kimbong. After all, according to the women, Dewa admits that the cattle belong to the Fon, and this explains Dewa's effrontery in calling the Fon by name, which is an abomination in this society that translates as the Grassfields of Cameroon. Dewa is also mindful that he and the Fon wield authority in the village, something that exonerates them from punishment. According to Nkfusai, Dewa is contemptuous of local traditional authority: "And when we said he would be hearing from Kwifon, he spat in our face and said the Fon had . . . the Kwifon" (15), or emasculated this cult.

The insistence of the women that Dewa must leave the village because of the destruction made by his cattle is opposed by the Fon because he too is an accomplice: "But they are people of this country. Some of your men own cattle. Will they too go?" (17). The Fon stresses that progress in the village is irrevocably tied to cattle, insinuating that he cannot exile graziers or stop the rearing of cattle. Even when he proposes to compensate the women for the destruction of crops, he wants only Dewa to bear the cost. In other words, he is determined to enrich himself to the detriment of this Fulani man: "You go muf two cow fo you nyun put tam for me nyun. Woman cow wey get leke three year so dat small tam dem get belle. You don hear fine, fine?" (18). He shamelessly gets the desired compensation of twenty thousand francs from Dewa, but he does not hand it to the women. He waits till they leave before saying to Dewa that "Give me de money. I go lef back pay them" (18), a statement that insinuates that the money would hardly reach the aggrieved women. He seems to justify his blighted conscience by sharing in Father Leo's opinion that any little money swindled must be invested in cattle. In that way, this scheming duo argues that their thievery would afford the villagers a good school, a health center, a motor road, and pipe-borne water (32). Nevertheless, Butake is wary of an economic system that is likely to enslave the majority, subjugating them to the selfish interests of the minority.[7]

In the culture of most parts of the North West Region of Cameroon, *Kwifon*, or the male secret cult, is responsible for the selection of Fons in fondoms, and also for the eviction from power of rulers who abuse their authority or engage in acts that are inimical to the well-being of their subjects. Members of this select group are believed to possess supernatural power which is used in resolving extraordinary problems. For instance, a tyrannical Fon or one that indulges in reprehensible behavior could be eliminated mysteriously. We notice that Butake dips into the folklore of a region that he knows at heart in order to indicate that even in rural traditional societies, there is a system of checks and balances in place, and he questions why such a practice cannot be adopted on the national or even continental level, given that most leaders in Africa are prone to misuse of authority.

As earlier pointed out, the group *Kwifon* acts as a guardian of tradition and morality in *Lake God*, particularly against the arbitrary rule of the Fon. It is made up of seven men who have as responsibility the enthronement/dethronement of Fons and the overseeing of the welfare of villagers. Faced with the intransigence of Fon Joseph to make sacrifices to the lake god and the Fon's belligerent attitude to this cult, *Kwifon* is compelled to assemble outside its sanctuary in the palace. Immediately after casting cowries, Shey Bo-Nyo predicts that disaster will afflict the village as intimated by the boiling lake water. We are told that, once every year and under the guidance of *Kwifon*, the Fon performed sacrifices in the lake. Regrettably, according to Kibow, a *Kwifon* member, with the enthronement of a Christian Fon the issue of libation has been proscribed, and the result is upheaval in the land: "Two years after the Fon banished Kwifon, / The lake god was again hungry for sacrifice" (41).

When *Kwifon* converges at the Fon's palace to address the problems confronting the land, the Fon not only reprimands the men for being irresponsible, but he also threatens the cult: "I have no use for Kwifon. And if you want to start trouble again, you know what happened last time" (42). In fact, the Fon undermines the power in the hands of this dreadful group that is capable of cowing anybody in the land. He is determined not to lead this group for sacrifices on grounds that its practices are heathen. Moreover, he warns that if *Kwifon* persists in its resolve to make sacrifices to the lake god, he would send the police after it. Before leaving the palace, *Kwifon* admonishes the Fon about the consequences of his behavior: "You will never have peace/ Because you have denied your people peace. / Your ancestors will never allow you respite/ Because you have ruined the land. / You are destroying the people" (44).

The following day, the Fon and his wife, Angela, suffer from insomnia. He is troubled by nightmares, one of which involves him and Father Leo in a dungeon. Amidst a tumultuous whirlwind marked by screams and thunder, the Fon is snatched by *Kwifon*. As Father Leo and Angela scramble to his rescue, they are intimidated by loud noises and they later crumble to the ground. Undoubtedly, *Kwifon*, the supreme and most feared authority in the land, has inflicted revenge on the Fon and his crony, Father Leo. Interestingly, it would seem that this calamity is not the work of *Kwifon* alone, but the result of an irate lake god that smites everything in its path, including members of *Kwifon*. Listen to the testimony of Shey Bo-Nyo: "As I staggered downhill towards the homesteads, / My first encounter was with the sacrificial train: / The seven pillars of Kwifon, the Fon in their midst, / Their faces buried in the earth for terror, in awe" (56). Therefore, the Fon's unwillingness to cooperate with *Kwifon* in ensuring the welfare of the village causes the decimation of the population.

As a sequel to *Lake God*, *The Survivors* deals with the problems confronting the survivors of the disaster orchestrated by the lake god. Old One, Tata, Mboysi and others undergo harrowing experiences of deprivation and psychological torture before a callous military man. Officer, the symbol of brutality in the play, arrests people on trumped-up charges of tax evasion. He terrorizes survivors of the lake catastrophe by routinely pointing his gun at them. His language is replete with threats: "He knows only two words: Stop! Silence!" (63). As Old Man laments, Officer's third word is the sound "Kpo" that is emitted from his (Officer's) gun. Officer personifies corruption and he acts kindly only when he gets sexual gratification from Mboysi. In fact, the survivors know that in order to overcome hunger and thirst, they need to trade Mboysi for favors from Officer. The ruling society, epitomized by Officer, is so morally repellent that it does not hesitate to seek personal aggrandizement at the disfavor of the helpless citizens.

Like the Kadiye in Wole Soyinka's *The Swamp Dwellers*, Officer feeds fat on the food reserved for the survivors: "A carton of cooking oil . . . Two bags of rice . . . One hundred kilogrammes of onions . . . A bag of mbonga from fishermen" (71). He doles out bits of these items to women like Mboysi provided that they satisfy his carnal desires. Listen to how he flatters the helpless Mboysi: "Your voice is like a drum, playing on my heart" (72). Officer could be symptomatic of the military and civilian officials that enriched themselves at the expense of the victims of the Lake Nyos explosion of August 21, 1986 in Cameroon. Financial, health, and food assistance destined for the survivors was unceremoniously confiscated by powerful, rapacious administrators.

In order for Officer to perpetuate the exploitation of the survivors, he has to circumscribe them to a specific location thereby justifying the reception of aid on their behalf. Old One's observation is pertinent: "So the people are sending those things, thinking that they are going to many survivors, and Officer is keeping the things for himself and his people. And giving us very little, because we don't know" (78). Mboysi is also aware that Officer is exploiting them and her, precisely, for his selfish, animalistic desires (78). Nevertheless, Old One is engaged in a moral warfare with Officer by refusing to eat the food that Mboysi gets from him. This symbolic gesture is a repudiation of the avarice and moral bankruptcy of Officer. In the same vein, Mboysi's crushing of the contents of the knapsack given her by Officer and her attempt to tear off the dress received from him could be seen as a subtle denunciation by Butake of the greed of Officer and, by implication, those in governance in Cameroon or Africa.

Unfortunately, Officer persists in his nefarious activities because he receives orders from above (81), meaning that he is protected against persecution by scheming military and administrative officials. However, in a sudden change of fortune, Mboysi takes possession of Officer's gun and fires it at him and then performs a victory dance. Regrettably, she is shot dead by other military men and, through her death, there is the likelihood of perpetuating the vicious cycle of evil masterminded by Officer. It would seem that her daring attack on him is not sufficient to stem the culture of corruption and evil. In this regard, Butake appears to suggest that it would need collective and sustained will if his society is to be purged of the corruption that has eaten up its fabric.

The issue of moral decadence in *The Survivors* is taken up in *And Palm Wine Will Flow*, which is the story of a headstrong ruler who clings to power despite the objections of his subjects. His reign is characterized by several injustices as he expects everybody to obey his dictates or suffer the consequences. Powerful as he may seem, the Fon's obsession with power is stopped by the *kibaranko*. It is before this awe-inspiring masked spirit that Gwei confesses that he and other loyalists collaborate to kill opponents of the Fon. The play pits, in the view of Nkengasong, the spiritual forces of the land against the tyrannical Fon who brings misery to the land. Through spirit possession, both the *kibaranko* and the earth-goddess overcome the Fon by ushering in a new order.[8]

Put simply, the *kibaranko* in *And Palm Wine Will Flow* is an avenger of justice in Ewawa. Its mission, as stated by Shey Ngong, is essentially the rendering of retribution in a palace fraught with criminality: "Let their heads be crushed like pumpkins/ And their brains be licked by the dogs! Let their bones crack and their members/ Be torn each from the other until they lie" (105). In other words, the purpose of the *kibaranko* is to cleanse the palace by dislodging tyrants like the Fon. By burning down the palace, it aims to stop tyranny. It could be inferred that the people of

Ewawa and, by extension, several dictatorial rulers in Africa are enjoined to govern collectively, in the spirit of democracy and not through the whims and caprices of power-drunk individuals.

Butake revisits the issue of misrule in the plays *Shoes and Four Men in Arms* and *Dance of the Vampires,* an indication of his preoccupation with good governance. Both plays explore the question of dictatorial rule. However, while *Shoes and Four Men in Arms* is focused on a military regime, *Dance of the Vampires* is centered on a monarchical government. Another significant difference in the plays is that while the one attempts to conceal evidence of brutality, the other explains how individuals employ various reprehensible ways to stay in power. Ultimately, both regimes totter toward collapse in the face of mounting opposition. Both plays also castigate arbitrary rule and use the symbols of shoes and vampire to express disapproval.

The pile of shoes in *Shoes* symbolizes not only the brutality of the army against unarmed civilians, but also indicates the number of dead and wounded from the high-handedness of the army against civilians protesting against tyranny, as exemplified in First Soldier's question: "Does this pile of shoes not tell you a story?" (127). Evidence of excessive use of force by the military against the civilians is again stated by him: "But I saw seven who had been operated because of bullet wounds. There is this girl lying there in a comma with a big wound in the back of her head. Somebody must have hit her with the butt of a rifle. I don't know if she can survive" (127).

In a desperate bid to hide incriminating evidence, soldiers take guard over the shoes of victims of military brutality. In this way, it would be difficult to use these items to corroborate charges of human rights abuse against the regime. Notice the panic and threats of death to which these soldiers are exposed if these shoes are missing: "Whatever you said, I want those shoes or I shoot both of you" (135) is the warning from Second Soldier. And when these shoes are ultimately stolen, the government is overcome by fear. In this regard, there is a radio communiqué decrying the disappearance of the shoes; a thorough house-to-house search is conducted for the missing shoes by soldiers; and a state of emergency is declared in the land. Here, there is the impression that Butake scoffs at the reaction of the government that imposes a curfew simply because of stolen items. Stated differently, the regime appears ignorant of its priorities, or at worst, uses this incident as an alibi to institute terror in the land. As a result, when the search for shoes is in progress, the soldiers rape women and torture men.

We notice that it is the same tendency to consolidate power that makes Psaul Roi in *Dance of the Vampires* seek membership in the vampire cult. Instead of this group acting as a check on the authority of Roi, he wants to be part of it thereby making him supreme with nobody to challenge his grip on power. He uses money and influence to subject the vampire club to his authority. Now as a leading vampire, his desire for power and influence cannot be buckled up. Unfortunately, immediately after he becomes chief vampire, several calamities hit the land. This is how Nformi sums up Roi's rule: "So he became high priest and chief vampire. That did not only signal the end of the vampire cult but also the beginning of a long list of calamities which ended with the massacre in the market place and the fleeing of people to foreign lands" (168). It is salutary that Psaul Roi's initiation into the vampire club culminates in his overthrow by Nformi. His loss of authority constitutes an indictment of leadership, especially in African countries, where most presidents pro-long their stay in power primarily through the complicity of the army. Because of their long tenure in office, some of these leaders consider themselves monarchs as the constitution is routinely toyed with, con-stantly under revision in order to make some of them life presidents.

In arguably his masterpiece, *Lake God*, Butake interpolates symbols in this drama to articulate his contention that those who need to be con-scientized are essentially the minority urban, political and bureaucratic elite. This group, according to him, has confiscated the power and wealth of the majority, and are using both for egoistic reasons.[9] Butake's plays not only interrogate some of the political, social, and economic injustices of his society, but also envisage ways like protest or rebellion to resolve some of these evils. Whether drawing from mythic imagination or from contemporary social scene, he makes his dramatic universe scathing com-mentary on contemporary social life in Cameroon, in particular, and Afri-ca, in general. His main concern, as Shadrach Ambanasom elucidates, is with irresponsible political leadership, unconscionable dictatorial rule, corruption, immorality, and the abuse of power.[10] Butake's symbols of the *Fibuen*, *Kwifon* and cattle in *Lake God*; Officer in *The Survivors*; *kibaran-ko* in *And Palm Wine Will Flow*; shoes in *Shoes and Four Men in Arms*; and vampire in *Dance of the Vampires* amply illustrate his preoccupation with oppression and exploitation, and suggestions about how to overcome these evils.

NOTES

1. Bole Butake, *Lake God and Other Plays* (Yaoundé: Editions CLE, 1999) 4. Further references to Butake's plays shall be taken from this edition and shall be cited in parenthesis henceforth in this chapter.

2. Northrop Frye, "Levels of Meaning in Literature." *The Kenyon Review* 12.2 (Spring 1950), 246–50.

3. Kelly A. Parker, *The Continuity of Peirce's Thought* (Nashville: Vanderbilt Univer-sity Press, 1998), 6.

4. Susan Diduk, "The Civility of Incivility: Grassroots Political Activism, Female Farmers, and the Cameroon State." *African Studies Review* 47.2 (September 2004), 30.

5. Diduk 33.

6. John Nkemngong Nkengasong, "Butake and Aristophanes: Libidinal Strategies and the Politics of the Traditional Woman," http://sookmyung.tongkni.net/admin/issue/upfileen (Accessed 12 December 2014).

7. Kashim Ibrahim Tala, "Economic Individualism and class consciousness in Bole Butake's *Lake God*." *The Nassau Review* 5 (1989), 86.

8. John Nkemngong Nkengasong, "Wole Soyinka and Bole Butake: Ritual Dramaturgy and the Quest for Spiritual Stasis." *Language, Literature and Identity*. Eds. Paul Mbangwana, Kizitus Mpoche, and Tennu Mbuh (Gottingen: Cuvillier Verlag, 2006), 75.

9. Bole Butake, "The Dramatist at Work: My Theatre Work Is Aimed at the Urbano-Politico-Bureaucratic Elite in Cameroon." *Theatre and Performance in Africa—Intercultural Perspectives*. Ed. Eckhard Breitinger (Bayreuth: Bayreuth African Studies Series, 2003), 101.

10. Shadrach A. Ambanasom, "Half a Century of Written Anglophone Cameroon Literature," http://www.eduartawards.org (Accessed 19 November 2013).

EIGHT

From Spoken to Texture

Orality in Lake God

The relationship between oral and written literatures of Africa is intertwined granted that written African literature usually draws inspiration from its oral counterpart. Once derided by Western critics as preliterate and anthropological, oral literature has taken center stage in African literary expression. Although the constituents of oral style, namely, communalistic ethos, unexaggerated prominence of the individual within his society, the utilization of proverbs, the use of stock characters in parabolic situations, the supernatural, praise names, and metaphors, as advanced by Chinweizu, Onwuchewka Jemie, and Ikechukwu Madubuike in *Towards the Decolonisation of African Literature*, may appear essentialist in the sense that not all African cultures manifest the same breadth and depth of sophistication, these critics, at least, identify important aspects of orature. The transition from the oral form to the written template is often done through transmutation, a process whereby the writer inscribes his or her text within the myths and folklore that constitute the tapestry of oral literature. As a result of the interplay between oral and written literature, Emmanuel Obiechina points out that a new "synthesis takes place in which characteristics of the oral culture survive and are absorbed, assimilated, extended, and even reorganized within a new cultural experience."[1] This chapter intends to demonstrate that the play *Lake God* exemplifies Bole Butake's seamless incorporation of elements of oral literature in his drama, as he interpolates proverbs, divinations and other elements of orality in his work. Butake's enterprise not only lends cultural signification to his play but also adds depth to his characterization and meaning.

By orality, we are referring to the creative chants, epic poems, musical genres, folktales, myths, songs, legends, recitations, proverbs, life histories or historical narratives, repetitions, riddles, tongue-twisters, and word games that constitute the artistic reservoir of a people. These different artistic modes are usually transmitted by word of mouth or performed live by (un)skilled performers. In a sense, oral literature is simply "literature delivered by word of mouth"[2] and this can take several forms like chants, proverbs, and folktales. Oral literature functions as the distinctive parent of written literature because it is "both reservoir and repertoire of traditions, models, and norms to which the critics allude and which define the literature as African."[3] By its nature, oral literature, as observed by Abiola Irele in *The African Imagination: Literature in Africa & the Black Diaspora*, continues to thrive in Africa because most Africans identify with it and it "represents that form of expression to which African sensibilities are most readily attuned."[4] Indigenous poetics are fundamental in written literature in that writers strive, according to Obiechina in his essay "Narrative Proverbs in the African Novel," "to create works that will endure by drawing upon their living oral tradition to enrich forms, techniques, and styles received through literate education."[5] Consequently, creative writers delve into native folktales, fables, incantations, rituals, and other forms of oral expression to not only ground their artistry within specific sociocultural matrices but also to create refreshing art.

Among the prominent elements of orality in *Lake God* are proverbs, honorific greetings, cults, rituals, divinations, and visions. To begin with, proverbs, as Chinua Achebe famously defines them in *Things Fall Apart*, are the palm oil with which words are eaten. Proverbs encapsulate wisdom and are often associated in traditional African societies with the wise and elderly. It is in this regard that the Narrator in *Lake God* bemoans the situation of famine and disease that have struck the land and underscores the point that in time of hardship, relatives and neighbors are those whom we can rely on for assistance: "When death strikes, it is your kinsman / That mourns with you. It is he / Who wipes the tears from your eyes/ And brings comfort to your heart."[6]

Prior to the catastrophe that strikes the land, Shey Tanto, a prescient member of the *Kwifon*, a male secret cult, expresses his fears, in the following proverb, about the uncertainty in which the land is embroiled: "The things that are happening in this land are pregnant" (20). Tanto's observation is highly suggestive given the fact that, unlike the previous Fon who believed in the local tradition and routinely performed sacrifices to appease the gods of the land, the current Christian Fon is deeply entrenched in Christianity at the expense of traditional religion. He undermines several aspects of traditional religion like divination and propitiation, an oversight that most likely generates death and destruction in the land. To compound the situation, the Fon's romance with materialism (he owns most of the cattle that destroy crops) and the welfare of the people constitutes an explosive issue in that the *Fibuen* women, a female secret cult, embark on a sex war on the men, an action that precipitates a headlong collision between *Kwifon*, on the one hand, and the Fon, on the other.

The Narrator in *Lake God*, like the few survivors of the explosion that kills many people in the land, is helpless and desperate for assistance as attested to in the following metaphor: "I am the weather-beaten owl/ Scampering into dark grove at the approach of / Dawn, fearful of the terrible silence / Descended over the land" (7). The images of an owl and darkness underscore the sense of despondency in the survivors as well as the extent of the tragedy that has struck the land.

As the play *Lake God* unfolds, the women, most of whom are members of the *Fibuen*, are furious about the cavalier attitude of the Fon in the face of the increasing destruction of crops by cattle. Fueled by a feeling of conspiracy on the part of the Fon toward their misery, the women beat and tie up Dewa, a Fulani cattle owner, and carry him to the palace. The women's action, according to Kinchin, one of the Fon's guards, is an attempt to desecrate the land given the unwillingness of the Fon to resolve the problem of cattle encroaching farms.

Notwithstanding their grievance on the Fon, the women are aware that they still have to show respect and loyalty to him in the form of honorific titles. Thus, in greeting the Fon, they prostrate and ululate in front of him, gestures that are typical of the people of the Grassfields of Cameroon. The Fon is eulogized in such honorific titles as lion, leopard, and elephant in order to vaunt his awe and authority across the land. For example, Nkfusai, a member of the *Fibuen*, makes the following comment about the Fon: "Who pounces on his own kind just to prove he is a leopard!" (16). Throughout the discussion between the Fon and the women, he is constantly addressed by the women as *Mbe*, an appellation reserved only for royalty in the North West Region of Cameroon where the play is set.

Interconnected with royalty is the idea that a traditional ruler in the Grassfields of Cameroon is expected to be polygamous, being capable of marrying many wives in order to demonstrate the masculinity and leadership acumen of the ruler. Unfortunately, this is not the case of the Christian Fon Joseph, who is only married to one wife, Angela, who is unable to bear offspring. The Fon's insistence on monogamy is challenged by the *Fibuen* women who request him to wed several women so as to ensure succession in case of vacancy. For her part, Angela's reluctance to welcome a co-spouse, in the eyes of the *Fibuen* women, manifests her greed and unwillingness to let other women share in her "fortune."

Another important element of orality that Butake inscribes in *Lake God* is divination, which is the ability of trusted diviners or mediums to predict events or read the future through observation or decipher meaning from (un)natural phenomena. With regard to *Lake God*, Shey Bo-Nyo regularly conducts divinations by casting his cowries and kola nut on the ground in order to divine the future. In one of his séances, he prognosticates before Shey Tanto, another *Kwifon* member, that: "Worse things are yet to come. Did you notice that all the cowries have been falling on their bellies?" (22). Bo-Nyo insists on the urgency for the Fon to lead the people in a sacrifice to the lake god failing which disaster will strike the land: "If the Fon does not offer sacrifice to the lake god as his fathers before him always did, we can get ready for the worst" (22).

However, Fon Joseph now stands in the way of the age-old practice of traditional religion by not only proscribing, for example, divination, but also, through his guards, brutalizing and humiliating Shey Bo-Nyo, the priest of the lake god that is believed by the natives to ensure their well-being. The Fon's guards mercilessly pounce on the diviner, leaving him aching from pain and licking his body like a dog (20). The torture and shame inflicted on the diviner symbolize the rejection, by the Fon, of the authority and sovereignty of *Kwifon* in the land. In addition, the disgrace incurred by the priest of the lake god gestures toward the calamity that will befall the Fon, when he will be supernaturally killed by *Kwifon*.

It is interesting to observe that the starvation that has engulfed the land is an incipient sign of the hard times that await the Fon. Regrettably, he turns a blind eye to this unfortunate situation, preoccupied by his propensity to enrich himself by swindling money and cattle from Fulani grazers like Dewa. The Fon's intransigent attitude toward the pleas of the *Fibuen* women that cattle grazers must leave the land galvanizes female opposition to his rule. Ma Kusham, leader of the women's cult, administers the oath of sealed lips to her compatriots, a ritual that is often used by women of the Grassfields of Cameroon to draw attention to their grievances. In the particular situation in *Lake God*, the amazon Ma Kusham instructs her womenfolk not to disclose the decision of a sex war which the women are waging on the men. She performs a ritual that involves sprinkling of water and placing broomsticks between the lips. The injunction to secrecy must be adhered to otherwise, in the words of Ma Kusham, "If my mouth discloses what my ears have heard in this gathering, may my tongue swell and fill my mouth with dumbness" (25). It does not take long for us to notice the consequences of the decision of the women as evidenced when Fisiy, a village man, laments in front of his compatriots that the women are sexually starving the men: "Has any of you called his wife to your bed in the last week? Ever since the Fibuen was heard?" (28).

In the face of the stiff opposition from both *Kwifon* and *Fibuen* toward his rule, the Fon seeks protection from his Christian religion represented by Father Leo and the latter is apparently powerless to protect him. The Fon does not only engage in verbal altercations with members of the men's and women's cults, but he is also seemingly psychologically and supernaturally harassed by these cults. It is worth mentioning that *Kwif-on*, for instance, in the North West Region of Cameroon is a highly dreaded cult because of the belief held by most people in this part of the country that this group is imbued with superhuman powers. Thus, when the Fon is experiencing nightmares, he confides his fears in Father Leo and attributes his uneasiness to the mischief of *Kwifon*. Moreover, according to the Fon, his late father has been reprimanding him for the troubles in the land: "I have been having some terrible dreams. I have been seeing my late father . . . and he is always blaming me for the trouble in the village" (38). Father Leo attempts in vain to squash the eerie feeling welling up in the Fon by ascribing his discomfort to fever, to which he prescribes camoquine.

Faced with the stubbornness of the Fon to initiate a ritual ceremony to avert an impending disaster, Shey Bo-Nyo defies the Fon's authority by leading *Kwifon* to the lake god, whom he enjoins to protect the land. Accompanying *Kwifon* is a masked figure, carrying the sacrificial items intended for the lake god. While Bo-Nyo performs libations, he invokes the spirits of the land to watch over the living:

> We are meeting in this sacred grove of the lake god
> Because the land is no longer the land
> You illustrious ancestors handed over to us.
> Kwifon is in exile; and the women of this land
> Are waging war against their men-folk
> Because the Fon, our Fon, the Fon you gave us;
> The Fon we thought you gave us, has sold the land.
> To strangers and rearers of cattle. (39)

The iteration of the words "the Fon" by the priest is a typicality of oral literature, a repetition which Butake weaves into his craft to show the significance of the Fon's actions to the welfare of the people under the Fon's rule. As he appeases the lake god, Bo-Nyo requests for patience, peace of mind, and wisdom from him. However, when he casts his cowries to foretell the future, he envisions calamity to the land: "No use to read the stars./ The waters of the lake boil!" (40). The die appears cast for the land given that, according to Kibow, one of the seven pillars of *Kwifon*, the present Fon, unlike his predecessor, has refused to lead the people in sacrifice. Contrary to the case of the former Fon who often led the people in sacrifices to the lake god, the present Christian Fon has not only forbidden these sacrifices on grounds that he considers them pagan, but has also banished *Kwifon*, the custodian of this ritual. As a result, according to Kibow, the lake god is unleashing havoc on the land because it has not been pacified.

The persistent boiling of the lake for four days, in the opinion of Shey Tanto, is a dire warning from the lake god for the inhabitants to heed their responsibility. Although Tanto associates the sweltering lake with the fury of the lake god, the Fon ascribes the unusual activities in the lake to the rains and thunder (43). According to the Fon, only a charlatan like Shey Bo-Nyo, the priest of the lake god, will read supernatural significa-tion to the happenings in the lake. The Fon is dogged in his Christian belief, dismissing the pleas of *Kwifon* for him to lead the people in a ritual ceremony on grounds that he does not worship idols and so cannot rec-oncile his Christianity with what he regards as the anti-Christian mindset of his people in appeasing spurious gods. He deliberately ignores the point that most of his compatriots are practitioners of traditional religion, which seeks to ensure a balance "between human society and natural forces in the universe—sometimes visible, sometimes invisible."[7] Going by the word of the priest of the lake god, dreadful consequences await the Fon because of his neglect of traditional religion:

> You will never have peace
> Because you have denied your people peace.
> Your ancestors will never allow you respite
> Because you have ruined the land.
> You are destroying the people.
> But Kwifon is alive yet.
> The land might still be saved,
> And the people too. (44)

As indicated earlier, the Fon seeks protection from Christianity in the face of the impending threat to his life and rule. Determined as he is to brush off the thought of revenge from the lake god, the Fon's nightmares put him in a paroxysm of fear. His wife, Angela, is also cowed by the unusual weather in the land and both she and the Fon are exhausted from want of sleep and are nervous about their future. This is what the Fon says in regard to his anxiety:

> Last night, for instance, I dreamt that I was with Father Leo in a dun-geon. He kept telling me not to worry. Then, suddenly, he was no longer there. I was all alone; in that dark dungeon. I was so frightened I started shouting and groping about in the terrible darkness. A little while later, I saw a tiny light flickering in the distance. As I stumbled towards the light, I soon saw the shadow of the late Fon, my father. Then the light disappeared and I woke with a start. (45)

The prose language of the Fon underlines the depth of his apprehension with regard to his safety and authority in the land. The dream is symbolic on several levels. First, it presages the impending doom awaiting him, when he will lose his life. Second, the dream demonstrates that his full embrace of Christianity to the exclusion of traditional religion is proble-matic. As the political and spiritual leader of his people, he is expected to welcome the dissenting beliefs and ways of life of his people. By stigma-tizing traditional religion in favor of Christianity, he alienates several of his people, who are adherents of traditional religion and perceive it as their *modus vivendi*.

For her part, Angela has a presentiment of doom that looms in her mind: "But I have a terrible feeling something is going to happen" (45). Even though she is a Christian like the Fon, her mind is more eclectic than that of her husband. She, like most African Christians today, is aware that in order to be successful, rulers must be tolerant toward the different political, social and spiritual perceptions of those whom they govern. This partly explains her chastisement of the Fon, when she queries him for fully embracing Christianity without concern for traditional religion: "I beg, lef me da white man palaver. You ought to listen to your people sometimes" (45).

In spite of the disdain shown toward him and his god, Shey Bo-Nyo still nurses the hope that disaster could still be averted. This explains his penultimate attempt to appease an irate god, when he goes to the shores of the lake in an endeavor to forestall the looming catastrophe or, at least, mitigate its consequences. Unfortunately, the priest's mission is belated:

> When the messenger of death finally emerged
> From the depths of the dark waters
> With strict instructions to sow desolation,
> I was there on my knees pleading for mercy.
> Give them one last chance. I cried.
> Listen, Kwifon is on the way with sacrifice.
> But in his impatience and terrible wrath,
> He knocked me out of his way. (56)

Men, women, children, the Fon, and *Kwifon* are swept away, according to Shey Bo-Nyo, by a vengeful god. The priest of the lake god and the few survivors of the catastrophe seek refuge in the neighboring village of Ewawa. They trudge to the rhythm of the mourning song, *Mangvun*, and the bit of the musical instrument, *Ngem*, which both delineate the profundity of the crisis in the land as well as the perilous future of the survivors.

While it may be rational to attribute the misfortune in the land to natural causation or, precisely, severe weather, it is also plausible to apportion blame on external forces. In other words, there is a conflation of scientific and supernatural explanations to the tragedy. To this end, the Fon is convinced, like his mentor Father Leo, that the trouble in the land is due to thunder and heavy rains whereas Shey Bo-Nyo blames a vengeful lake god. For his part, Man, one of the few survivors of the catastrophe, indicts the Fon for romanticizing with Christianity to the complete disregard of traditional religion, or for conspiring with an alien religion against the interest of its local equivalence:

> The Fon, father and guardian of all the land,
> Offspring of a long line of illustrious ancestors,
> The fountain-head of tradition

And shelter of all the land.
The Fon made alliance with strangers
And called Shey Bo-Nyo mad.
He turned a deaf ear to Kwifon,
Supreme and most feared authority in the land.
And now this. (53)

A definitive explanation of the cause of the tragedy that befalls the village is beyond the purview of this inquiry. Nevertheless, the study of the elements of oral literature in *Lake God* has not only showcased the rhetorical skills of Butake's native Noni people, but also demonstrated how to create literature that experiments with new forms of expression and how contemporary African artists, as Anthonia C. Kalu states, can fashion new literary tastes that illuminate "a world view consistent with that of lived traditional and contemporary African experience."[8] Hence, through the artistic frame of oral literature that essentially englobes proverbs, honorific greetings, cults, rituals, divinations, and visions, Butake, in *Lake God*, recreates the world view of traditional Noni people, in particular, reimagining the political, cultural, historical, and psychological thoughts of his people or Africans as they grapple with the complexities of modern science and Christianity that interrogate their belief system. In other words, Butake's literary enterprise represents an endeavor to preserve in print form certain aspects of his culture, particularly at a time of the totalizing influence of Western culture. Concomitantly, the playwright, through this creative template, renders dynamic his characterization as well as equivocates meaning. It has also been shown that the boundaries between orality and written literature are not dense, but permeable and negotiable. Thus, Butake, in this particular play, is not retracing an elusive past, but recasting and semiotizing it in order to mediate the present.

NOTES

1. Emmanuel Obiechina, "Narrative Proverbs in the African Novel." *Oral Tradition* 7.2 (1992), 197.

2. Isidore Okpewho, *African Oral Literature: Backgrounds, Character, and Continuity* (Bloomington: Indiana University Press, 1992), 3.

3. Craig Tapping, "Voices Off: Models of Orality in African Literature and Literary Criticism." *Ariel: A Review of International English Literature* 21.3 (July 1990), 75.

4. F. Abiola Irele, *The African Imagination: Literature in Africa & the Black Diaspora* (Oxford: Oxford University Press, 2001), 30.

5. Obiechina, 199.

6. Bole Butake, *Lake God and Other Plays* (Yaoundé: Editions CLE, 1999), 7. Further references to Butake's plays shall be taken from this edition and shall be cited in parenthesis henceforth in this chapter.

7. Rose Ure Mezu, *Chinua Achebe: The Man and His Works* (London: Adonis & Abbey Publishers, 2006), 190.

8. Anthonia C. Kalu, "African Literature and the Traditional Arts: Speaking Art, Molding Theory." *Research in African Literatures* 31.4 (Winter 2000), 60.

NINE

Character and the Supernatural in *Lake God*

Bole Butake constructs *Lake God* against a background of traditional Noni and Christian belief systems that appear to impinge on the actions of his protagonists. Butake's dramatic framework makes it questionable for us to discuss his main characters in isolation of the culture that informs their behavior and actions. In other words, his play represents a textual tapestry of traditional Noni sociocultural norms as well as beliefs of the Christian religion, which seeks to subvert traditional religion. While we may blame the downfall of the Fon and Father Leo, for example, on their intransigent and confrontational attitude, it is also plausible to explain their tragedy to their nonrespect of traditional Noni religion like performing sacrifices to the lake god, as well as their embrace of Christianity. In this chapter, we submit the argument that, although Butake's tragic heroes have their individual failings that significantly contribute to their downfall, a more meaningful appreciation of the fate of the leading characters must also take into consideration traditional Noni sociocultural and Christian matrices; issues that partly explain the complexity of Butake's characterization and equivocate interpretations of the fate of the protagonists.

The play *Lake God* is the story of a catastrophe that befalls a village apparently because of a gas explosion in a lake, or because of the failure of the people to appease an irate god supposedly lurking in the lake. Written immediately after the gas explosion in Lake Nyos in Menchum, Cameroon, in August 1986 that killed over 1,700 people, in addition to cattle and other livestock, Butake, in *Lake God*, interrogates both scientific and local explanations given about the explosion. Historically, whereas the Cameroon government and scientists attributed the Nyos explosion to the release of accumulated carbon dioxide at the bottom of the lake,

107

conspiracy theorists still hold that the explosion resulted from a bomb that was tested by foreign scientists with the complicity of the government. Butake feeds off this controversy in *Lake God*. Through the Fon and Father Leo, representing the Christian religion, and Shey Bo-Nyo and Shey Tanto, symbolizing traditional Noni religion, Butake gives contrary explanations about an explosion that decimated several villages in Menchum. While the first group of characters in *Lake God* appears to ascribe the calamity to toxic gas from a lake, the second group attributes the misfortune to the refusal of the Fon to lead the village in sacrifices to the lake god.

NEW HISTORICISM AND CULTURAL MATERIALISM

Conceived by American critic Stephen Greenblatt, New Historicism generally refers to a renewed interest, initially among American critics in the early 1980s, in discussing literary works as historical and political documents. Leaning toward feminism and Marxism, this critical lens takes a questioning view of the past and analyzes the consumption and status of literary productions. Important to New Historicism is the assumption that the inquiry being done may not be objective, but the issue of the past is dictated by the concern with the present. Put differently, New Historicism, unlike deconstruction which engages in philosophical abstraction and uncertainty, examines literature as a cultural artifact. This is precisely because art is not created in a vacuum; it is not simply the creation of an individual, but that individual is fixed in time and space, responding to a community of which he or she constitutes an important element.

Cultural Materialism, the British equivalent of New Historicism, aims to examine how texts reflect or critique an ideological position. In other words, this approach looks at how a text relates to the specific institutions of cultural production. History, in this sense, encompasses politics, power, ideology, authority and subversion. British cultural materialists perceive texts as offering opposition to authority. Seen from a holistic perspective, New Historicism and Cultural Materialism take an eclectic view of criticism by historicizing literature, or considering literary texts as part of a historical culture. Such a rethinking of history brings flexibility to literature by breaking down the artificial boundaries separating both. The relationship between history and literature makes both complement each other as each helps in explaining the other.

TRADITIONAL NONI SOCIETY AND THE CHRISTIAN RELIGION

The supernatural can be defined as something that exists beyond nature, or not subject to explanation according to scientific and natural laws; something that is neither physical nor material. It can be imaginary, mysterious, or capable of generating unreasoning. Religion, whether Christian or traditional, plays a significant role in explaining the world view of a people, their day-to-day life, future, and afterlife. Thus, it is only against the backdrop of the traditional Noni and Christian belief systems that we can convincingly appreciate the behavior, actions and fate of Butake's protagonists in *Lake God*.

Noni representations of the supernatural, like most traditional societies in the North West Region of Cameroon, are evident in their traditional religion, cultural beliefs, mythology, and divination, as well as the relationship between the living and the living dead. These perceptions of the world translate into a traditional Noni vision of the interconnectedness between the physical and the spiritual, in a way that a rupture in the delicate balance between these spheres can possibly result in confusion or even catastrophe. Thus, the traditional Noni world view seems holistic, embracing the living, the departed, and the unborn.

Traditional Noni religion has to do essentially with the supernatural, the performance of rituals to the ancestors involving libations using important sacrificial items such as chicken, palm wine, cowries, and kola nut. Among the Nonis, there is also the practice of traditional medicine, which is the prerogative of certain individuals who are believed to be endowed with the ability to cure illnesses such as madness, epilepsy, or even prevent individuals from being preternaturally harmed by their enemies, witches, or wizards.

Indeed, the world view of traditional Noni people is mediated by the physical and the spiritual universe. This is because, as Emmanuel Obiechina rightly argues in *Culture, Tradition and Society in the West African Novel*, the world view of a traditional West African village is dependent on the interplay of the physical, seen world and the invisible world of the gods/goddesses, spirits, ancestors, magicians and witches. Typically, people in oral, traditional societies generally tend to "explain their problems, as well as all mysterious phenomena, through recourse to a theory of supernatural or mystical causality."[1] All the more so because of the belief that spirits inhabit the forests, air, hills, and lakes. Moreover, in traditional Noni cosmology, life does not end with death; some departed members of families are believed to be spiritually in touch with the living, especially in times of misfortune or disaster. This explains the practice of paying respect, through various libations, to the ancestors who are believed to watch over the actions of the living.

Furthermore, traditional Noni people believe in divination and diviners are thought to possess special skills that enable them to divine supernatural aspects of life. In fact, within the traditional Noni society, diviners are considered special because of the belief that they are imbued with, according to Sean Sheehan and Josie Elias, a "combination of intuitive knowledge and acquired skills built over a lifetime of living and working in the community"; the impression that diviners enjoy magical and supernatural powers is "reinforced by the way in which divination is achieved through special means" such as mystical revelations, inheritance, or intuition.[2]

The Nonis also show great respect to traditional institutions such as the *Fondom* and *Kwifon*. While the Fon is perceived within the Grassfields of Cameroon as the custodian of traditional authority, *Kwifon* acts as a check on the powers of the Fon given that it "sees and hears everything. It is said to have as many eyes as a basket has holes."[3]

In *Lake God*, for instance, the Fon is referred to in various Homeric epithets by the women of the *Fibuen* and men of the *Kwifon*—lion, leopard, and elephant, which are metaphors for authority, royalty and power in the Grassfields of Cameroon. Additionally, Noni people are not allowed to greet the Fon by hand or to touch any of his accoutrements of power such as staff, calabash and stool. This is partly because the Fon is believed to enjoy extraordinary or mystical powers.

Like traditional Noni religion, Christianity appears to incorporate aspects of the supernatural in its doctrine, which insists on the immaculate conception of Mary and the resultant birth of Christ, or the symbolic ritual of baptism that is associated by Christians with the cleansing of sin. Also, the story is told in Ezekiel 13:18–21 about how women used handkerchiefs to trap the souls of men and later killed them. Such a narrative challenges our rational understanding of things, bordering occasionally on the mysterious and incomprehensible.

As Angulu Onwuejeogwu aptly states, be it in a Christian or non-Christian setting, anything that is conceived beyond natural existence can be referred to as "super nature" or supernatural.[4] In this regard, Emile Durkheim seems to synchronize Christian and traditional perceptions of life in terms of their religious practices (prayers, purifications, sacrifices, dances, and songs), which he regards as a combination of ideas that express the world.[5]

Just like his traditional counterpart, the Fon, Father Leo commands considerable respect within the village, especially among Christian converts. This explains why he can rebuke the *Fibuen* women for indulging in what, according to him, are demonic practices. He warns them to refrain from traditional religion (reenacting the women's cult) otherwise they would rot in hell. Father Leo's behavior is typical of that of early missionaries to Cameroon who expected Christian converts, like the Fon and Angela in *Lake God*, not simply to read the Bible, but also "to study European culture, abandon their 'native' ways, engage in employment of a European nature (implying abandonment of such traditional pursuits as hunting and gathering), and generally become 'civilized.'"[6]

THE PROTAGONISTS AND THE INFLUENCE
OF THE SUPERNATURAL

Lake God opens against a highly suggestive background—a whirlwind rising and colliding with darkness—as the audience is exposed to a macabre spectacle of corpses strewn across the stage, victims of the apparent wrath of the lake god. According to Shey Bo-Nyo, diviner and priest of the lake god, ascribing this calamity to toxic gas is erroneous as this would rouse the anger of an already vengeful god.[7] He insists that the land has been beset by calamity because of the Fon's flirtation with Christian religion at the expense of its traditional counterpart.

While Father Leo emphasizes the merits of Christianity (health centers and schools) over traditional religion, Shey Bo-Nyo points out that the land can only be saved from impending disaster by seeking recourse to traditional religion, represented by the lake god. At the same time, the Fon is harangued by the *Fibuen*, the women's cult, on grounds that he, going by the word of Dewa, a Fulani cattle grazer, has abolished the *Kwifon*, the men's cult, because of his romance with Christian values. The Fon now considers *Kwifon* pagan and morally repugnant to his Christian rule. It is, therefore, against the contending forces of traditional Noni religion and Christianity that the character traits of the Fon, Father Leo, Shey Bo-Nyo and Angela are played out.

The Fon's opposition to traditional Noni religion is unequivocal: he proscribes the offering of sacrifices to the lake god, something which the *Fibuen* women believe can render Angela, the queen, fertile; he refuses to marry a second wife, stating that Christianity outlaws polygamy; and he returns to their parents the brides that his late father had taken in marriage. In addition, he is recusant as evidenced in his refusal to inherit any of the widows of the late Fon as required by Noni tradition. The Fon's attitude is contrary to that of the late Fon, who successfully reconciled Christianity and traditional religion by encouraging the construction of a school and a Church, for example, in his village while simultaneously performing traditional rites like propitiating the lake god. However, according to Ma Kusham, leader of the *Fibuen*, things "of the white man have brought suffering to the land" (25) in her reference to the rule of the Fon.

For his part, Fisiy, one of the village men, reprimands the Fon for being discriminatory by embracing Western values to the detriment of traditional ones: "The Fon is the one who is breaking the laws and destroying the land in the name of this new religion brought by Father Leo" (30). Unfortunately, the Fon's zealous embrace of Christianity only serves to polarize his village in terms of religious ideologies.

Hard as the Fon may attempt to extirpate any thoughts of traditional religion in his mind, he is still haunted by it. He admits to Father Leo, his patron and parish priest of the village, that he, the Fon, is having visions of his late father, in which the departed Fon reproaches him for bringing chaos and suffering to the village through his neglect of traditional practices. In other words, the Fon is superstitious and his projected Christian identity cannot entirely erode his lingering traditional-oriented religious predisposition. In this connection, Father Leo occasionally reprimands him for comparing the priest of the lake god to that of the Christian religion: "How dare you, Fon! How dare you make such a comparison!/ In spite of all my efforts? In spite of all that I have done for you? You/ even dare to make reference to idols in my presence?" (10).

Father Leo makes an interesting exegesis of the Fon's distraught mind, which he ascribes to symptoms of malaria. He gives a prescription of camoquine as a cure to the Fon's malaise. Through prayers, Father Leo further requests the Christian God to save the Fon from any trouble. It is interesting to note the apparent rivalry here between traditional religion and Christianity in the sense that while the Fon appears to be psychologically affected by traditional religion for his negligence toward it, Father Leo's Christian religion seeks to offer the Fon protection against its traditional counterpart. Unknown or overlooked by both Father Leo and the Fon is the fact that Shey Bo-Nyo is seeking the security of traditional religion against what to him are the insidious actions of the Fon, activated by the Christian religion. In fact, Butake, through this incident, prods the warped conscience of the Fon, bringing it alive and enabling the Fon to undergo introspection and assess his role in the tragedy that befalls the village.

Although the Fon is briefed by *Kwifon* about the disaster looming over the village, he dissociates himself from traditional religion by giving a scientific explanation to the seemingly unusual occurrences noticed in and beyond the lake. According to the Fon, the rumblings noted in the sky and the sporadic peals of thunder are the result of the rainy season; he avers that Shey Bo-Nyo's divination about an incipient calamity in the land is the product of the priest's hallucinating mind. The Fon also cites Father Leo to attest to the view that Shey Bo-Nyo is an impostor, a quack priest seeking self-glorification by fomenting fear in the villagers. As a result, the Fon does not yield to *Kwifon's* request that he immediately lead the people in sacrifice to the lake god. Against the pleas of *Kwifon*, representing traditional religion, the Fon counters their threat of disaster by invoking Christianity, insisting on the point that, as a Christian ruler, he does not partake of idol worshipping. Put differently, as *Kwifon* seeks protection of the land from traditional religion, the Fon retorts that the Christian God had already saved the land. However, Shey Tanto, leader of *Kwifon*, warns the Fon that because the Fon has renegaded traditional religion, the Fon will never know respite.

Upon casting his cowries to divine the fate of the village, Shey Bo-Nyo predicts that misfortune will strike it because the gods are angry with the villagers for neglecting, through the Fon, annual ritual ceremonies. His efforts to persuade the recalcitrant Fon to appease the irate lake god through sacrifices are in vain because the Fon considers this practice barbaric and heathen (21). For their part, the *Fibuen* women, as earlier indicated, envision in the propitiating ritual an opportunity to render the queen productive in order to ensure succession at the throne.

In *Lake God*, Father Leo essentially functions like the Fon's alter ego as he encourages the ruler to be steadfast in his hostility to the practices of the *Kwifon* and *Fibuen*. Because of his bloated ego, Father Leo undermines the women's revolt against their husbands, describing it as an "uncoordinated action by a handful of ill-disciplined village women" (36). In line with his bellicose attitude, he also orchestrates the banning of *Kwifon* because he considers their practices conflicting with those of the Christian religion, and inimical to progress within the land. Furthermore, in a strongly worded address to women during a doctrine class, among whom are members of the *Fibuen*, Father Leo castigates them for starving their husbands of food and sex; for imploring the Fon to chase grazers and their cattle because of the destruction of crops; and for being contemptuous to the Fon by refusing to sell food to Angela, the Fon's wife. He insists that if these women do not recant their actions, they will "suffer the pangs of everlasting fire" (33). Thus, the priest uses the might of his Christian God to forecast hard times to anyone associated with traditional religion.

Paradoxically, the Fon and Angela are among the first victims of the conflict between Christianity and traditional religion. Immediately after his verbal warfare with the *Kwifon*, the Fon is harassed by nightmares, which bring to the fore the clash between the dominant religions in the land, or the different religious perceptions of Father Leo and the Fon, on the one hand, and the late Fon and Shey Bo-Nyo, on the other:

> And I am still having those terrible dreams. Last night, for instance, I dreamt that I was with Father Leo in a dungeon. He kept telling me not to worry. Then, suddenly, he was no longer there. I was all alone; in that dark dungeon. I was so frightened I started shouting and groping about in the terrible darkness. A little while later, I saw a tiny light flickering in the distance. As I stumbled towards the light, I soon saw the shadow of the late Fon, my father. Then the light disappeared and I woke with a start. (45)

In a bid to overcome his beleaguered mind, the Fon looks forward to requesting Father Leo to secure, through prayers, his palace against any baneful action on the part of *Kwifon*. Angela, however, thinks differently, stating her presentiment about something sinister happening to the village. Although she is an educated headmistress of a school, Angela is prudent enough to avoid a rift between traditional religion and Christianity by respecting, to a certain extent, certain practices of both religions. Challenged by the Fon about her Christian faith that instead leads her to be superstitious, Angela's response is poignant as she affirms that the Fon ought to incarnate elements of both religious streams: "I beg, lef me dat white man palaver. You ought to listen to your people sometimes" (45). Like Pa Matiu in Kenjo Jumbam's *The White Man of God*, a Cameroonian novel, Angela's opinion appears to be that of realism in the play as she clearly symbolizes many of today's African Christians who comfortably embrace elements of both Christianity and traditional religion.

When Angela expresses her apprehension about the lake boiling, the Fon attempts to allay her fears by attributing the cause to the effect of the rainy season. However, the Fon's explanation is problematized in the events that accompany the stormy weather—thunder peals and heavy downpour. Thereafter, Angela coughs loudly and is hypnotized momentarily as the Fon is led away by *Kwifon*. As Father Leo braces himself to these apparently uncanny events, intent on using the police to rescue the Fon, there is a deafening sound that plunges the village into a cataclysm. While these occurrences can be traced to the consequences of the poisonous gas released by the lake, it is also possible to blame a wrathful god apparently lurking beneath the lake. In this regard, according to Shey Bo-Nyo, the lake god has lost its patience with the village for not offering it sacrifices and, as a result, has unleashed its vengeance on the people:

> I was there on my knees pleading for mercy.
> Give them one last chance, I cried.
> Listen, Kwifon is on the way with sacrifice.
> But in his impatience and terrible wrath,
> He knocked me out of his way. (56)

Shey Bo-Nyo's analysis of the tragedy that has befallen the land is also shared by Man, one of the survivors, who attributes the calamity to the Fon's repudiation of traditional religion.

LAST WORD

In a sense, Butake, in *Lake God*, engages both traditional Noni and Christian religions to foreground the character of his protagonists: on the one hand, he dramatizes through the supernatural the intransigence and bigotry of the Fon, and, on the other, he brings to focus the opinionated, belligerent and rigid state of mind of Father Leo. Far from the extreme position of these two characters stands Angela, who is broad-minded or catholic in her world view while Shey Bo-Nyo, though a traditionalist, is eclectic in mind and more likely to tolerate the practice of Christianity provided that it does not stand in the way of traditional religion. After all, he spends most of his time in the grove of the lake god, without taking umbrage at the charge, from his detractors, that he is delusional. A plausible reason for Butake's integration of the supernatural in this particular play is that the issue of religion is so overwhelming to the protagonists and is of a collective nature that necessitates a mythic approach to it.

Moreover, Butake primarily employs the supernatural to explore the psychology of his protagonists. This is clearly evident in the tormented states of mind of the Fon and Father Leo when the one has nightmares and the other is agitated when he learns about the capture of the Fon by *Kwifon*. There is no evidence in the play that Butake subscribes to the supernatural, or that he prefers one form of religion to the other. Through a supernatural frame, he essentially underscores the flaws of his protagonists such as rashness and bigotry (towards indigenous practices) in the Fon, and overzealousness and myopia on the part of Father Leo. In fact, interpretation of events and the actions of the characters in *Lake God* can sometimes be problematic considering traditional Noni cosmology and the Christian religion that appear to inform events and cloud meaning. Beyond the showcasing of traditional Noni society, Butake's use of the supernatural in *Lake God* amplifies characterization, reinforces major themes, equivocates interpretation, and enhances his readability.

NOTES

1. Emmanuel Obiechina, *Culture, Tradition and Society in the West African Novel* (Cambridge: Cambridge University Press, 1975), 39.

2. Sean Sheehan and Josie Elias, *Cultures of the World: Cameroon* (New York: Marshall Cavendish Benchmark, 1999; 2011), 83.

3. Lorenz Homberger, ed., *Cameroon: Art and Kings* (Zurich: Museum Rietberg, 2008), 72.

4. Angulu Onwuejeogwu, *The Social Anthropology of Africa* (London: Heinemann, 1975), 222.

5. Emile Durkheim, *The Elementary Forms of Religious Life*. Trans. Karen E. Fields (New York: The Free Press, 1995), 430.

6. John Mukum Mbaku, *Culture and Customs of Cameroon* (Westport, Connecticut: Greenhood Press, 2005) 62.

7. Bole Butake, *Lake God and Other Plays* (Yaoundé: Editions CLE, 1999), 7. Further references to *Lake God* shall be taken from this edition and shall be cited in parenthesis henceforth in this chapter.

TEN

Conclusion and Butake's Legacy

Today Anglophone Cameroon literature is rich and diverse, unlike in 1970s and 1980s, when its forte was the short story, encouraged considerably by the late Professor Bernard Fonlon,[1] Anglophone Cameroon literature has embraced and experimented with virtually all genres of literature. This laudable endeavor has been largely facilitated by publishing houses such as Editions CLE, Langaa Common Initiative Group, and Miraclaire, with hundreds of published works. Such literature continues to probe issues of marginalization, culture, and politics and Butake has been a leading figure in this initiative. In recognition of his indefatigable contribution to the development of culture in Cameroon, Butake was awarded a medal on January 19, 2016, by the minister of Culture, in a ceremony that was attended by an enthusiastic crowd.

Like a committed writer, Butake envisions his role as bringing awareness, through drama, to some of the ills of his society such as exploitation, discrimination, corruption and power abuse. The thoughts of D. H. Lawrence, in a letter dated January 22, 1925, in which he argues that the artist should not remain indifferent to societal vices, but his or her works should make people "either run for their lives, or come under the colours" and the artist "should be in among the crowd, kicking their shins"[2] can be applied to Butake given the latter's concern with the inequalities and injustices of his society. This explains Butake's practice of popular theater, in which the problems of the community are dramatized and solutions suggested, in many parts of Cameroon.

The book, *Art and Political Thought in Bole Butake*, has sought to place Butake's dramatic creations within a specific sociopolitical time frame. Although Butake's primary artistic universe is his Noni ethnicity, the study has demonstrated how this society can convincingly correlate to Cameroon, in particular, and Africa, in general, because of the highly suggestive referents in Butake's drama. Butake essentially uses his native Noni society as a creative template to make political commentary. Stated differently, the events recounted in the plays strongly resonate with sociopolitical situations in Cameroon or Africa. Before independence in the 1960s, there was the lament on the extent of exploitation and brutality perpetuated by the European colonial powers on the continent of Africa. However, it would seem that over fifty years after independence, the plight of Africa has hardly changed, confirming the saying that the more things change, the more they remain the same. This adage is pertinent with regard to Cameroon, where there are blurred lines between the colonial and postcolonial administrations in terms of authoritarianism. After all, according to Jean-Germain Gros, "It is scarcely an exaggeration to say that the story of post-colonial Cameroon is the story of centralized authority in Yaoundé trying to impose itself on the rest of the country, sometimes by force sometimes by inducement, and using foreign policy [especially French] to consolidate domestic power."[3]

Granted that an artist hardly creates in a vacuum, we have established correspondences between scenarios dramatized in Butake's works with events in Cameroon or Africa. He historicizes notable events in Cameroon as well as textualizes certain aspects of its culture. For example, the Lake Nyos disaster of 1986, the struggle for multi-party politics in the 1990s, and the role of *Kwifon* and *Takumbeng* are all disasters and/or events still fresh in the minds of Cameroonians. Thus, Butake's drama constitutes a clever collage of history and culture.

In other words, the study has analyzed Butake's drama along the tropes of politics and culture, signposting important symbols such as lion in *And Palm Wine Will Flow* and cattle in *Lake God* as pointers to the degree of power abuse and corruption that are entrenched in contemporary Cameroon and, by extension, Africa. Butake does not contend himself with identifying the pitfalls of his society, but, as a committed writer, he envisions protest as a possible pathway to curbing systemic misuse of authority. By creatively reimagining his society and foregrounding issues of politics, culture, and ethics, Butake challenges his audience to rethink and reassess values that can revitalize humanity in terms of justice and well-being. Stated differently, the dramatist appeals to the dominant groups of society to reassess the policy of subjugating other people to various political indignities and, to the dominated, the message appears to be one of emboldening them to challenge the status quo in order to reap the benefits of what legitimately is theirs.

While essentially decrying political ills such as corruption and self-centeredness, Butake also interrogates the question of female marginalization by showing, for example, in *Lake God*, how women are disabused by men in leadership positions. He juxtaposes men and women as they confront the problem of cattle destroying crops. Through the Fon, he portrays the menfolk as egoistic and opinionated while the *Fibuen* women are depicted as responsible and dedicated, as the latter compels the former to appraise the leadership crisis in the land.

Even though this study has been primarily preoccupied with analyzing the political undertones of Butake's drama, there is still much to be explored with regard to his stagecraft, or, precisely, how he recreates oral elements of his Noni people, in particular, and the Grassfields of Cameroon, in general, in his dramatic universe. This is, to recall T. S. Eliot, Butake's objective correlative as Butake uses this artistic frame to vilify the wrongs of his society. The incorporation of traditional Noni beliefs and folklore in his art makes it distinct, fascinating and refreshing and these qualities enhance his readability.

As earlier pointed out, Butake's drama engages and instructs people from different facets of life: from underprivileged groups that perceive in his creative works alternative ways to challenging dictatorship and usurpation of civic rights and to literary pundits who are called upon to reevaluate and reargue his message within the ever-shifting politics and cosmos of Africa. In a sense, his drama will continue to engage audiences across the continent not only because of its aesthetics, but fundamentally because of the beacon of hope it holds out to the despondent and disempowered.

As pointed out earlier, this study of Butake's works does not pretend to be comprehensive or conclusive; indeed, its intent is to open up Butake's works and world to the outside world. The project has exposed the Cameroonian society to the world as Butake has used his artistic expression to diagnose a society replete with its own issues and problems. Indeed, the plays are not as bleak as many readers tend to see, for each play raises hopes of some future progress, albeit minor, for change is the only constancy in today's world.

As a gadfly of the people, Butake could not avoid playing the double role of a rebel/teacher and an entertainer. The former carried the burden of living perpetually in fear of persecution and abandonment and the latter the burden of respecting the norms and traditions of dramatic literature. And Butake did a remarkable work of combining both without being pedantic or preachy. What comes across as an aftertaste is the lingering feeling or impression of having watched, for example, a documentary of the Ewawa people in *And Palm Wine Will Flow* and the subversion of the people's identity and self-determination. It is a society in which the people have been rendered powerless, but not hopeless because the stirring hopes are kindled in the minds of the women who wield the secret power, but are not yet bold enough to assume this power in public partly because it is a patriarchal society. The Kwengongs and the Mboysis in *And Palm Wine Will Flow* will overthrow the Fons, but enthrone the Sheys under strict orders to run the society as a democracy not a dictatorship.

Though the men have apparently failed in Butake's dramatic universe, the women still want to give these men a second chance at leadership, for this is a society of second chances. In another domain, Butake's
plays are set at the crossroads between reality and art (fiction), where art
tends to reflect what is really happening in society. Hence, Butake moves
from the urban to the suburban and the country settings to reveal that
corruption, nepotism, and the abuse of power are not only reserved for
the urbanized society. The Fon, in the rural milieu, is a replication of the
magistrate and the lawyer in the urban setting, which brings a new dimension to the whole concept of culpability. The relegation of women to
secondary positions in the village is a microcosm of the relegation of
some ethnic groups on the political plane, which calls attention to the
pervasive nature of political discrimination and marginalization.

Indeed, Butake transfers political activism from the urban center to
the countryside or villages, where the fight for political change is not
adulterated by secretly nursed notions of the leaders who have their eyes
set on political positions and posts. In fact, the revolutionists are selfless
with the pretention to power, for when these women gain this power,
they simply hand it to the men. This is a shift in political power paradigm
against a backdrop where military takeovers have been planned by the
military personnel who replaced the civil leaders and declined to give
back power to the civilians. These are the projections that make Butake's
oeuvres prophetic and futuristic as he proposes a re-management of political power where the opposition leaders are not just fighting to replace
the entrenched political powers, but rather to become stewards of political change. It is not the fight for "our-time-now" politics, or in Cameroonian parlance "bellytics," but one prefixed on real change. For we have
witnessed failed governments, primarily in postcolonial societies, as a
replacement of one form of colonialism with another, a situation which
Franz Fanon bewailed unto his death.[4] Whether postcolonial governments are as (in)effective as colonial ones, the underlying impression is
that many who read Butake's plays see what is happening in Cameroon
or Africa as a reaction to some of the issues raised in the plays.

NOTES

1. Bernard Fonlon, as professor of African literature at the University of Yaoundé,
conceived and edited a scholarly review, *ABBIA*, in which many budding Anglophone
Cameroon writers published their creative works.

2. *The Letters of D. H. Lawrence* Vol. 5 (1924–27). Eds. James T. Boulton and Lindeth
Vasey (Cambridge: Cambridge University Press, 1989), 201.

3. Jean-Germain Gros, "Cameroon in Synopsis" *Cameroon: Politics and Society in
Critical Perspectives*. Ed. Jean-Germain Gros (Lanham: UP of America, 2003), 21.

4. Frantz Fanon, *Toward the African Revolution* Trans. Haakon Chevalier (New
York: Grove Press, 1969). Also see Albert Mermmi, *The Colonizer and the Colonized*
(Boston: Beacon Press, 1965).

Select Annotated Bibliography on Bole Butake

Alembong, Nol. "Oral Traditions in Literary Imagination: The Case of Spirit Possession in Bole Butake's *And Palm Wine Will Flow*." *Anglophone Cameroon Writing 30*. Eds. Lyonga, N., Eckhard Breitinger & Bole Butake. Bayreuth: Bayreuth African Studies, 1993. 130–42. Print.

> Examines how Butake draws on oral tradition, particularly spirit possession, as an effective dramatic technique.

Ambanasom, Shadrach. *Education of the Deprived: A Study of Four Cameroonian Playwrights*. Yaoundé: Yaoundé University Press, 2003. Print.

> Demonstrates how women in Butake's drama are politically active as seen in their different actions such as protest and sex war to effect social change.

Breitinger, Eckhard. "Bole Butake's Strategies as a Political Playwright." *African Theatre: Playwrights & Politics*. Eds. Banham, Martin, James Gibbs, and Femi Osofisan. Oxford: James Currey, 2001. 7–17. Print.

> Butake's plays aim at politically educating the elite, with the goal that they rise up against an oppressive system of governance and implant a grassroots democracy.

———. "'Lamentations Patroitiques': Writers, Censors and Politics in Cameroon." *African Affairs*. Vol. 92 (1993): 557–75. Print.

> Projects Bole Butake as a daring writer who defies an oppressive political system to draw attention to the grievances of the masses.

Eyoh, Hansel Ndumbe. "Historicity and New Anglophone Cameroon Drama." *Anglophone Cameroon Writing* 30. 101–08.

> Portrays Butake's drama as one of social change or as a powerful instrument to conscientize people.

Jick, Henry and Andrew T. Ngeh. "The Moral Concept of Violence in African Literature: Bole Butake's Vision in *Lake God* and *And Palm Wine Will Flow*." *Humanities Review Journal* 2.2 (2002): 32–43. Print.

> The essay argues that Bole Butake recommends violence as a weapon to combat oppression in any society.

Ngwang, Emmanuel. "Literature as Politics: Revisiting Bole Butake's *Lake God and Other Plays*." *The Literary Griot* 14.1 & 2 (Spring/Fall 2002): 265–88. Print.

Establishes parallels between Butake's plays and Cameroon's political landscape and indicates how Butake faults the ruling government for its oppression of the masses. At the same time, the playwright aligns with the oppressed by appealing for change in the political apparatus.

Ngongkum, Eunice. "Revolutionary Discourse on Dramaturgy: Bate Besong's *Beasts of No Nation* and Bole Butake's *Lake God*." *Epasa Moto* 3.1 (2008): 171–87. Print.

Women in Butake's and Besong's drama do not contend themselves with decrying their plight, but they take steps toward calling attention to their problems.

Nkealah, Naomi E. "Challenging Hierarchies in Anglophone Cameroon Literature: Women, Power and Visions of Change in Bole Butake's Plays." Ph.D. Diss., University of Witwatersrand, 2011. Print.

Analyzes how women in Butake's plays construct power and its implications on issues of masculinity and feminism.

———. "Grotesque Manifestations of Power in *Dance of the Vampires* by Bole Butake." *Literator: Journal of Literary Criticism, Comparative Linguistics and Literary Studies* 34.1 (2013): 1–7. Print.

The article discusses Butake's *Dance of the Vampires* as a narrative of a nation and how political ideologies are conceived, especially in an oppressive system of governance.

———. "Memory, Expiation and Healing in Bole Butake's *Family Saga*." *English Academy Review* 27 (2010): 45–59. Print.

Analyzes how healing and reconciliation can be achieved in a postcolonial nation like Cameroon, which is characterized by linguistic and cultural diversity.

———. "Women as Absented Presences: Gender and Nationalist Discourse in Bole Butake's *Shoes and Four Men in Arms*." *English in Africa* 41.2 (October 2014): 95–114. Print.

Debates the role of women in political change in Cameroon and concludes that they play a peripheral part in politics because this arena continues to be male-dominated.

Odhiambo, Christopher. "Whose Nation? Romanticizing the Vision of a Nation in Bole Butake's *Betrothal Without Libation* and *Family Saga*." *Research in African Literatures* 40.2 (Summer 2009): 159–72. Print.

Demonstrates how Bole Butake romanticizes the concept of nation and nation-ness with regard to Cameroon, but his vision of nationhood is subverted by internal problems as well as colonialist machinations.

———. "Impotent Men, Energized Women: Performing Woman-ness in Bole Butake's Dramas." *Performing Gender in Arabia/African Theater: Between Cultures, Between Gender*. Ed. Mieke Kolk. Amsterdam: Intercultural Theatre Series, 2009: 165–80. Print.

Butake's plays illustrate how men have abused power in Cameroon and women are standing up to resolve some of the problems in the community.

Takem, John Tiku. *Theatre and Environmental Education in Cameroon*. Bayreuth: Bayreuth African Studies, 2005. Print.

Discusses how Butake draws from oral tradition to foreground a new political system that would replace the current oppressive regime in Cameroon, in particular, and Africa, in general.

Bibliography

Achebe, Chinua. *Things Fall Apart*. London: Heinemann, 1958; 2008. Print.

Aka, Emmanuel Aloangomo. *The British Southern Cameroons 1922–1961: A Study in Colonialism and Underdevelopment*. Plattville: WI: Nkemnji Global Tech, 2002.

Ambanasom, Shadrach A. *Education of the Deprived: Anglophone Cameroon Literary Drama*. Mankon, Cameroon: Langaa, 2010. Print.

———."Half a century of written Anglophone Cameroon Literature," http://www.eduartawards.org (Accessed 19 November 2013).

Armah, Ayi Kwei. *The Beautyful Ones Are Not Yet Born*. London: Heinemann, 1968. Print.

Asante, Molefi Kete. *Facing South to Africa: Toward an Afrocentric Critical Orientation*. Lanham, MD: Lexington Books, 2014. Print.

Ashuntantang, Joyce B. *Landscaping Postcoloniality: The Dissemination of Cameroon Anglophone Literature*. Mankon, Cameroon: Langaa, 2009. Print.

Banham, Martin, James Gibbs and Femi Osofsan. Eds. *The African Theatre: Playwrights and Politics*. Oxford: James Currey Ltd, 2001. Print.

Bigsby, Christopher W. E. *Modern American Drama: 1945–2000*. Cambridge: Cambridge University Press, 2000. Print.

Biya, Paul. *Communal Liberalism*. London: Macmillan, 1987. Print.

Boahen, A. Adu. *African Perspective on Colonialism*. Baltimore: The John Hopkins University Press, 1987. Print.

Bohannan, Paul and Philip Curtin. *Africa and Africans*. Fourth Edition. Prospect Heights, IL: Waveland Press, 1995. Print.

Boulton, James T and Lindeth Vasey. Eds. *The Letters of D. H. Lawrence Vol. 5 (1924–27)*. Cambridge: Cambridge University Press, 1989. Print.

Brannigan, John. *New Historicism and Cultural Materialism*. New York: St. Martin's Press, 1998. Print.

Breitinger, Eckhard. "Bole Butake's Strategies as a Political Playwright." *The African Theatre: Playwrights and Politics*. Eds. Martin Banham, James Gibbs and Femi Osofsan. Oxford: James Currey Ltd., 2001. 7–17. Print.

Butake, Bole. *Lake God and Other Plays*. Yaoundé: Editions CLE, 1999. Print.

———. "The Dramatist at Work: My Theatre Work Is Aimed at the Urbano-Politico-Bureaucratic Elite in Cameroon." *Theatre and Performance in Africa-Intercultural Perspectives*. Ed. Eckhard Breitinger. Bayreuth: Bayreuth African Studies Series, 2003. 101–4. Print.

Carby, Hazel V. *Reconstructing Womanhood: The Emergence of the Afro-American Woman Novelist*. New York: Oxford University Press, 1987. Print.

Champion, Ernest A. *Mr. Baldwin, I Presume: James Baldwin–Chinua Achebe: A Meeting of the Minds*. New York: University Press of America, Inc. 1995. Print.

Chinweizu, Onwuchewka Jemie and Ikechukwu Madubuike. *Towards the Decolonisation of African Literature*. Vol. 1. Enugu: Fourth Dimension, 1980. Print.

Diduk, Susan. "The Civility of Incivility: Grassroots Political Activism, Female Farmers, and the Cameroon State." *African Studies Review* 47.2 (Sept. 2004): 27–54. Print.

Doh, Emmanuel Fru. *Anglophone-Cameroon Literature: An Introduction*. Lanham, MD: Lexington Books, 2015. Print.

Durkheim, Emile. *The Elementary Forms of Religious Life*. Trans. Karen E. Fields. New York: The Free Press, 1995. Print.

Durning, Alan Thein. "Supporting Indigenous Peoples." *State of the World: A World Watch Institute Report on Progress Toward a Sustainable Society.* Ed. Linda Starke. New York: W. W. Norton & Company, 1993. 80–100. Print.

Ehlen, Patrick. *Frantz Fanon: A Spiritual Biography.* New York: The Crossroad Publishing Company, 2000. Print.

Emecheta, Buchi. *Destination Biafra.* Oxford: Heinemann, 1994. Print.

Fanon, Frantz. *Black Skin, White Masks.* New York: Grove Press, 1952. Print.

———. "Letter to the Resident Minister 1956." *Search for New Forms of Culture.* Ed. Jo G. Leadingham. Acton, Mass: Copley Custom Publishing Group, 1999. 387–89. Print.

———. *The Wretched of the Earth.* New York: Grove Press, Inc. 1968. Print.

———. *Toward the African Revolution.* Trans from French by Haakon Chevalier. New York: Grove Press, 1967. Print.

Foncha, John Ngu. Letter. 9 Jun. 1990. Print.

Parker, Northrop. "Levels of Meaning in Literature." *The Kenyon Review* 12.2 (Spring 1950): 246–62. Print.

Geschiere, Peter. *The Perils of Belonging: Autochthony Citizenship, and Exclusion in Africa & Europe.* Chicago: University of Chicago Press, 2009. Print.

Gros, Jean-Germain. "Cameroon in Synopsis." *Cameroon: Politics and Society in Critical Perspectives.* Ed. Jean-Germain Gros. Lanham, MD: University Press of America, 2003. 1–31. Print.

Harris, Joseph E. *Africans and Their History.* 2nd Edition. New York: Meridian, 1998. Print.

Homberger, Lorenz. Ed. *Cameroon: Art and Kings.* Zurich: Museum Rietberg, 2008. Print.

Hooks, bell. *Ain't I a Woman: Black Women and Feminism.* Boston, MA: South End Press, 1992. Print.

Irele, F. Abiola. *The African Imagination: Literature in Africa & the Black Diaspora.* Oxford: Oxford University Press, 2001. Print.

Jacobson, Jodi. "Closing the Gender Gap in Development." *State of the World: A World Watch Institute Report on Progress Toward a Sustainable Society.* Ed. Linda Starke. New York: W. W. Norton & Company, 1993. 61–79. Print.

Joyce, James. *A Portrait of an Artist as a Young Man.* Cambridge: Cambridge UP, 2004. Print.

Jumbam, Kenjo. *The White Man of God.* London: Heinemann, 1980. Print.

Kalu, Anthonia C. "African Literature and the Traditional Arts: Speaking Art, Molding Theory." *Research in African Literatures* 31.4 (Winter 2000): 48–62. Print.

Khapoya, Vincent B. *The African Experience: An Introduction.* Upper Saddle River, NJ: Prentice Hall, 1998. Print.

Kodjo, Edem. *Africa Tomorrow.* Trans. E. B. Khan. New York: Continuum, 1987. Print.

Labang, Oscar C. *Riot in the Mind: A Critical Study of John Nkemngong Nkengasong.* Yaoundé: Miraclaire Publishing, 2008. Print.

Lazarus, Neil. "(Re)turn to the People: Ngugi wa Thiong'o and the Crisis of Postcolonial African Intellectualism." *The World of Ngugi wa Thiong'o.* Ed. Charles Cantalupo. Trenton, NJ: African World Press, 1995. Print.

Maimo, Sankie. *I am Vindicated.* Ibadan: Ibadan University Press, 1959. Print.

Martin, Phyllis M. and Patrick O'Meara. Eds. *Africa.* Third Edition. Bloomington: Indiana University Press, 1995. Print.

Mbaku, John Mukum. *Culture and Customs of Cameroon.* Westport, CT: Greenhood Press, 2005. Print.

Memmi, Albert. *The Colonizer and the Colonized.* Boston: Beacon Press, 1967. Print.

Mezu, Rose Ure. *Chinua Achebe: The Man and His Works.* London: Adonis & Abbey Publishers, 2006. Print.

Miller, Arthur. "The Family in Modern Drama." *The Theater Essays of Arthur Miller.* Eds. Robert A Martin and Steven R. Centola. New York: Da Capo Press, 1996. 68–85. Print.

Mukong, Albert. HRDG's letter to the Prime Minister of Cameroon: /11/01 *SCNCFOR-UM Re:[africadaily3]* 5:47 p.m. 1–4. Print.

Musinga, Kwo Victor Elame. *The Tragedy of Mr. No Balance*. Bamenda, Cameroon: Langaa Research & Publishing CIG, 2008. Print.

Ngugi wa Thiong'o. *Devil on the Cross*. London: Heinemann, 1982. Print.

Nkengasong, John Nkemngong. "Butake and Aristophanes: Libidinal Strategies and the Politics of the Traditional Woman,"http://sookmyung.tongkni.net/admin/issue/upfileen(Accessed 12 December 2014).

———. "Interrogating the Union: Anglophone Cameroon Poetry in the Postcolonial Matrix." *Journal of Postcolonial Writing* 48.1 (2012): 51–64. Print.

———. "Wole Soyinka and Bole Butake: Ritual Dramaturgy and the Quest for Spiritual Stasis." *Language, Literature and Identity*. Eds. Paul Mbangwana, Kizitus Mpoche and Tennu Mbuh. Gottingen: Cuvillier Verlag, 2006. 73–82. Print.

Obiechina, Emmanuel. *Culture, Tradition and Society in the West African Novel*. Cambridge: Cambridge University Press, 1975. Print.

———. "Feminine Perspectives in Selected African Novels." *Nwanyibu: Womanbeing and African Literature. Number I*. Eds. Phanuel A. Egejuru and Ketu.Katrak. Trenton, NJ: African World Press, 1997. 33–46. Print.

———. *Language and Theme: Essays on African Literature*. Washington, DC: Howard University Press, 1990. Print.

———. "Narrative Proverbs in the African Novel." *Oral Tradition* 7.2 (1992): 197–230. Print.

Okpewho, Isidore. *African Oral Literature: Backgrounds, Character, and Continuity*. Bloomington: Indiana University Press, 1992. Print.

Onwuejeogwu, Angulu. *The Social Anthropology of Africa*. London: Heinemann, 1975. Print.

Osborne, John. *Look Back in Anger*. London: Macmillan, 1956. Print.

Pallister, Janis L. "From La Noire De . . . to Milk And Honey: Portraits of the Alienated African Woman." *Nwanyibu: Womanbeing and African Literature*. Number 1. Eds. Phanuel A. Egejuru and Ketu H. Katrak. Trenton. NJ: African World Press, 1997. 135–45. Print.

Panichas, George A. Prefatory Note: *The Politics of Twentieth-Century Novelist*. New York: T.Y. Crowell, 1974. i–xviii. Print.

Parker, Kelly A. *The Continuity of Peirce's Thought*. Nashville: Vanderbilt University Press, 1998. Print.

Peirce, Charles S. *Peirce on Signs: Writings on Semiotics*. Ed. James Hoopes. Chapel Hill: University of North Carolina Press, 1991. Print.

Ramiez, Victoria. "The Impact of Colonialism on African Women's lives in Novels by Marian Ba, Buchi Emecheta, and Ama Ata Aidoo." Frankfort, Kentucky: SIRAS, April 12, 2000. 144–49. Print.

Sandbrook, Richard. *The Politics of Africa's Economic Stagnation*. New York: Cambridge UP, 1985. Print.

Sartre, Jean-Paul. "Introduction." *The Colonizer and the Colonized*. By Albert Memmi. Boston: Beacon Press, 1967. xxi–xxiv. Print.

Schorer, Mark. *Sinclair Lewis: An American Life*. New York: McGraw-Hill Book Company, 1961. Print.

Shakespeare, William. *Macbeth*. Ed. Robert S. Miola. New York: W. W. Norton & Company, 2004. Print.

———. *Othello*. Ed. Michael Neil. Oxford: Oxford UP, 2006. Print.

Sheehan, Sean and Josie Elias. *Cultures of the World: Cameroon*. New York: Marshall Cavendish Benchmark, 1999; 2011. Print.

Soyinka, Wole. *Collected Plays*. Vol. 1. London: Oxford UP, 1973. Print.

Stratton, Florence. *Contemporary African Literature and the Politics of Gender*. London: Routledge, 1994. Print.

Stryker, Richard and Stephen N. Ndegwa, "The African Development Crisis." *Africa*. 3rd Edition. Eds. Phyllis Martin and Patrick O'Meara. Bloomington: Indiana University Press, 1995. 375–94. Print.

Sudarkasa, Niara: "The 'Status of Women' in Indigenous African Societies." *Women in Africa and the African Diaspora*. Eds. Rosalyn Terborg-Penn, Sharon Harley, and Andrea B. Rushing. Washington, DC: Howard University Press, 1987. 25–41. Print.

Takougang, Joseph and Milton Krieger. *The African State and Society in the 1990s: Cameroon's Political Crossroads*. Boulder, Colorado: Westview Press, 1998. Print.

Tala, Kashim Ibrahim. "Economic Individualism and Class Consciousness in Bole Butake's *Lake God*." *The Nassau Review* 5 (1989): 80–87. Print.

Tapping, Craig. "Voices Off: Models of Orality in African Literature and Literary Criticism." *Ariel: A Review of International English Literature* 21.3 (July 1990): 73–86. Print.

Transparency International. http://www.transparencyinternational.org 1998, 1999, and 2001.

Tuana, Nancy. *The Less Noble Sex: Scientific, Religious, and Philosophical Conceptions of Woman's Nature*. Bloomington: Indiana UP, 1993. Print.

Uwakweh, Pauline Ada. "Female Choices: The Militant Option in Buchi Emecheta's *Destination Biafra* and Alice Walker's *Meridian*." *Nwanyibu: Womanbeing and African Literature*. Number 1. Eds. Egejuru and Katrak. 47–60. Print.

Walker, Alice. *Meridian*. New York: Harcourt Brace Jovanovich, 1976. Print.

Wallace, Karen Amyley. "The Black Female Presence in Black Francophone Literature." *Women in Africa and the African Diaspora*. Eds. Terborg-Pen, Sharon Harley and Andrea B. Rushing. Washington, DC: Howard University Press, 1987. 181–207. Print.

Welter, Barbara. "The Cult of True Womanhood, 1820–1860." *Dimity Convictions: The American Woman in Nineteenth Century*. Columbus: Ohio University Press, 1976. Print.

Index

About the Authors

Emmanuel N. Ngwang is a professor of English and director of the Quality Enhancement Plan (QEP) at Texas College in Tyler, Texas where he teaches English and literary studies. He obtained a B.A. and CAPES from the University of Yaoundé, (Cameroon) and an M.A. and Ph.D. from Central State University (now the University of Central Oklahoma) in Edmond and Oklahoma State University in Stillwater, Oklahoma, respectively. His interest in postcolonial literature has resulted in several single-article conference presentations and publications on Bole Butake's plays and Anne Tanyi-Tang. His research interests also embrace American immigrant literature and the whole gamut of African immigration to the United States, which have been published in book chapters and presented at several academic conferences. He is also chief editor of the *Journal of Educational Research and Technology (JERT)*, where he has equally published several articles on literature and immigration.

Kenneth Usongo holds a Ph.D. in comparative literature from the University of Denver, as well as a doctorate in English literary studies from the University of Yaoundé 1. Besides his books, *Ruminations of Ipome* and *The Rising Sun and Boma*, he has also published two dozen essays in English, postcolonial, and American literatures as journal articles and book chapters. He is associate professor of English at Texas College.